Martyn Cartledge

FLYING
FIRSTS

A month-by-month guide
to commercial aircraft maiden flights

To my late father, without whom my camera gear would still be in the dark ages, and to Sheena, my wife, without whose continuing support I would not be able to use that camera equipment to produce many of the images found in this book.

First published 2019

Destinworld Publishing Ltd
www.destinworld.com

British Library Cataloguing in Publication Data.
A catalogue record for this book is available from the British Library.

ISBN 978 1 9996470 4 9

Foreword

A maiden flight of a new aircraft type is always an historic and significant event. The culmination of thousands of hours of hard work in design, engineering and production, it is the final test to answer the ultimate question: 'Does it fly?' Even today, with sophisticated, computer-aided modelling, fly-by-wire systems, and test pilots having flown the aircraft 'virtually' in flight simulators, the level of anticipation for a first flight is palpable, should you be lucky enough to be in the presence of those who have helped the particular aircraft take to the sky.

In this book, acclaimed aviation photographer and journalist Martyn Cartledge takes an innovative look at first flights, month by month, throughout the year. It is an indispensable guide to maiden flights of commercial aircraft (both famous and rare) throughout history. The book is full of informative nuggets to ponder and digest. Why, for example, did the jumbo Boeing 747 and superjumbo Airbus A380 both fly in April, I wonder? And while the elegant Lockheed Constellation is most often associated with the red livery of TWA, in fact, the launch customer was Air France.

As I noticed on many a trip with Martyn when we were both covering aviation news, he has a keen eye for a great photograph and enthusiasm and knowledge of commercial air transport. Here, in this book, he also draws from many patient years of staking out airfields and airports, camera in hand, alternately shivering in the rain or boiling in the sun, to capture a rare aircraft.

Patience is needed because, despite the wonders of modern technology, the exact day on which an aircraft will fly is dependent on two things: a final thumbs-up from the flight-test team and something that is beyond anyone's control, the weather. Though the latest airliners can operate in all sorts of extreme conditions, on an important first flight the flight-test pilots and engineers will want to wait until there is reasonably good weather to reduce the variables and risk to a minimum. That said, the book is fascinating in that it shows how first flights are spread throughout the whole year – an indication perhaps of the underlying commercial pressures to race rivals into service and meet delivery deadlines.

However, nowadays nothing is left to chance, and long gone are the pioneering days in which a test pilot would casually 'kick the tyres and light the fires' and take a new aircraft aloft, perhaps wearing a hat, tie and smoking a pipe (and even that image may be more myth than reality as the greatest test pilots were always fully prepared, even if they appeared impossibly relaxed to observers). Today, the multinational teams, immense supply chains, global customers and media attention mean that a first flight is a tightly scripted affair – and the start of months and months of rigorous flight testing.

Consolidation in the aircraft industry has meant that familiar names such as de Havilland, Douglas, Tupolev and the like have all but disappeared, taken over or merged as the commercial airliner industry has coalesced around the twin gravities of the two giants – Airbus and Boeing. This mega duopoly and the immense costs of 'entering' this high-stakes global market has meant that clean-sheet airliner designs have become fewer and fewer. Indeed, it is said that it is easier for a nation to develop a space rocket programme than it is to develop a successful commercial airliner business. A successful and smooth first flight, then, is only part of the story.

These mergers, the high cost of entry and the plateauing of jet-engine efficiency mean that first flights of brand-new civil airliners have become rarer than in the past – with manufacturers concentrating on tweaking existing successful designs rather than taking giant leaps. However, the promise of hybrid/electric aviation, along with a new drive towards commercial supersonic flight, means that aviation is set to enter a new era of innovation. These new engine and power architectures, along with new materials, mean that the 'dominant configuration' of tube, wings and under-slung engines that have defined airliners since the 707 could be shaken up by more radical shapes making their first flights in future years.

AIRBUS A320NEO LIFTS OFF ON IT'S MAIDEN FLIGHT 25 SEPTEMBER 2014

This book takes a highly innovative approach to organising first flights using a month-by-month format, which will be of interest to the general reader, aviation enthusiast and aerospace professionals, as well as providing fodder for aviation pub quiz rounds (for example, what month links the Fokker F27 and Lockheed L1011 Tristar?) Some of the aircraft on these pages were huge commercial successes, others were sales flops. All deserve to be remembered as the expression of their designers' hopes and dreams that crystallise in that one moment when lift overcomes weight and an aircraft's wheels and the runway part company for the first time. I hope you enjoy reading it as much as I did.

Tim Robinson
Editor in Chief, Aerospace

Preface

I have been interested in Aviation for as long as I can remember, although sometimes it feels just like last week that it all began, but that is probably just my ageing brain. I have tried to get as many experiences as I can following this interest, which has seen me fly on a wide range of aircraft from a microlight to Concorde, passing through such oddities as the Scottish Aviation Twin Pioneer and the Airbus BelugaST.

To be the first to do something is an achievement that cannot ever be taken away and is therefore something to be cherished and proud of. Unfortunately, my closest claim to this type of honour is being the first-ever passenger on a particular Thai Airways A350, and not even their first at that, it was their fifth! Anyway, firsts in aviation, and in particular first-ever flights of aircraft and the first time they have done something for an airline or the industry as a whole, have been of particular interest to me over the years. I have collected memorabilia commemorating these events and followed the goings on around them. Running almost hand in hand with my interest in aviation has been my love of photography, and for nearly four decades (wow, am I that old?) I have been photographing the comings and goings at Manchester and other UK Airports. More recently though, I have been lucky enough to travel to some airports further afield and, in addition, witness first hand a number of aviation firsts. For some time I have been wondering just how to combine all my interests and make greater use of the thousands of images I have taken over the years. The result is what you hold in your hands today.

This book has been two years in the writing but decades in the making and is intended to both inform and entertain as it is a combination of an interesting read (at least I think so), a great collection of aircraft images (ditto) and a reference manual. You can even personalise it with your own first flight details.

This is my first-ever attempt at a book, although I have been writing features for (mainly) aviation magazines for well over a decade, as well as more recently launching an aviation-based website and blog. It has been quite a rollercoaster ride, particularly in terms of worrying over meeting deadlines and the amount of effort required to maintain the inertia and focus to keep going when the end never seemed to be getting any closer, despite the many hours sat at my keyboard. It has also been a challenge to balance the dissemination of the required information whilst keeping the text interesting and none repetitive. I guess you will be the final judge of whether I have succeeded in this or not!

Jane's All the World's Aircraft has been an invaluable document in the hope of ensuring that the details you see here are all correct. The world's aircraft manufacturers have been helpful in varying degrees, but it would be wrong of me to say who has helped the most and who hasn't! Tim Bernars-Lee needs a mention aswell, as without the internet this job would have taken a great deal longer.

Split into 12 chapters, one for each month, you can simply read it, look at the photos or check out a particular date important to you to see if anything happened on or around that day. At the back there are two appendices with every aircraft in the book listed, along with the date of their first flight. One is in alphabetical order and the other in chronological order, so whichever way you need the information it is readily available to you.

It would be lovely to hear what you have to say about this book, constructive feedback is always a hugely useful tool moving forward. Feel free to follow what I am up to via my website and blog at www.flywinglets.com, on my Facebook page with the same name or on Twitter @martynaspphotos, all of which can be used to make contact.

Most of all I really hope you enjoy the book.

All the best
Martyn

CONTENTS

Contents

JANUARY

Ilyushin IL62

The IL62 (NATO reporting name Classic) was the Soviet Union's first long-range jet airliner, purported to be the largest jet airliner when it was first flown. Mainly used by airlines in the old soviet bloc, it is similar in layout to the Vickers VC10. It was developed to replace the ageing TU114 turboprop aircraft on Aeroflot routes to places like New York, Tokyo, Cuba and the first international destination served, Montreal, in September 1967. The lengthy development programme was due to the aircraft's tendency to deep stall when the wings blocked airflow to the T-tail at high angles of attack. As was the case with many early soviet types, it required a large flight crew to operate it, in this case five.

Ilyushin went on to produce the IL62M, which had upgraded avionics, engines and 12 more seats, first flying in 1971.

Initially, IL62s were mainly for use by Aeroflot and the Soviet Air Force, but exports to friendly nations saw it operate in the liveries of airlines such as Cubana, CSA, CAAC and LOT. With the fall of the soviet republic, many aircraft found new owners such as Uzbekistan Airways, Domodedovo Airlines and Kras Air. Production ended in1993, by which time 292 had been produced. It is thought that Air Koryo in North Korea and RADA Airlines of Belarus have the only (non-VIP) aircraft still in service.

FIRST FACTS	
Launched	18/06/60
First Flight	02/01/63
Entered service	10/03/67 Aeroflot

STATS	
Length	61.21m (200ft 10in)
Height	17.60m (57ft 9in)
Wingspan	51.66m (169ft 6in)
Typical/Max seats	186/198
Number built	292

Tupolev TU204

The TU204 was designed as a replacement for the very successful medium-haul TU154. However, this aircraft did not do as well as its predecessor nor its competitor the Boeing 757. It was the first Russian airliner to have EFIS display screens and fly-by-wire flight controls. Although initially built with Russian-made Soloviev engines, Tupolev developed 'westernised' versions in an attempt to make the aircraft more attractive to the international market. The changes included Rolls Royce RB211 engines and Honeywell or Rockwell Collins avionics. Other operators included Cubana, Red Wings, Cairo Aviation and Aviastar. A number of variants were produced; the 214-300 was a shorter and longer-range version, making its first flight on 17 August, 2003 with Vladivostok Air taking the first delivery on 20 May, 2005. Other minor variants were introduced in later years. The aircraft never made a huge impression and there are now as many stored as there are active, making it a rare bird indeed.

FIRST FACTS

First Flight	02/01/89
Certification	12/01/95
First delivery	04/95
Entered service	23/02/96 Vnukovo Airlines

STATS

Length	46.14m (151ft 4 1/2in)
Height	13.87m (45ft 6in)
Wingspan	41.84m (137ft 3 1/4in)
Typical seats	214
Number built	83

Shorts Belfast

The Belfast was originally designed as a heavy freighter for the RAF; however, these aircraft only served with the Air Force for 12 years, and with Shorts failing to attract any other orders from civil or military customers they were made surplus. TAC Heavylift Airlines purchased five of these for commercial freight work. None are currently in regular service; however, one, thought to be the last flying example, is now stored at Cairns airport, painted all white, its fate unsure.

FIRST FACTS	
First Flight	05/01/1964
Entered service	20/01/1966 RAF

STATS	
Length	41.58m (136ft 5in)
Height	14.33m (47ft)
Wingspan	48.40m (158ft 9 1/2in)
Typical seats	N/A
Number built	10

Armstrong Whitworth AW.650 Argosy

This most unusual looking aircraft came about as a result of studies undertaken to produce a freighter for the RAF. However, the programme was never fulfilled, but after some commercial interest was shown the company decided to go ahead with this version as a private venture. The prototype, a series 100, made its first flight on 8 January, 1959 and was different to the original design in that it had doors at both ends of the central pod to enable easy loading and unloading and was designated AW.650.

The aircraft entered service in the USA with freight outfit Riddle Airlines, with BEA in the UK and SAFE Air in New Zealand being other early operators. Ironically, the main user ended up being the RAF, who needed replacements for existing freighters and paratroop platforms. 56 of the modified AW.660 were produced for this role.

Armstrong Whitworth also produced an updated version – the series 200 – which made its first flight on 11 March, 1964; however, only seven were ever built. After their original owners moved on to more modern equipment, the aircraft ended up with a number of freight operators around the world including Air Bridge Cargo, Elan Air, Aer Turas and Zantop, with the last being retired around 1991.

FIRST FACTS

First Flight	08/01/59
Entered service	1960 Riddle Airlines

STATS

Length	26.44m (86ft 9in)
Height	18.92m (29ft 3in)
Wingspan	35.05m (115ft)
Number built	17

Hawker Siddeley Trident

The de Havilland D.H.121 Trident, as it was originally known, is remembered for many firsts, but also for what was probably a missed opportunity.

In 1956 British European Airways (BEA) stated its requirement for a high-speed, jet-powered aircraft carrying (initially) 70 passengers up to 1,000 miles (1,600km), despite the airline's chief not really being a fan of jet aircraft. From the outset there were four companies bidding for the contract; however, after revising the spec of the aircraft, which included an increase to a maximum of 98 passengers, greater weight and increased range, it was de Havilland that got the nod.

Another first for the Trident was its ability to land completely automatically from approach through the flare, touchdown and roll out. Although scheduled to be in service by 1970, the aircraft performed the very first 'blind' landing of an aircraft in scheduled passenger service on 4 November, 1966 – a very useful piece of technology given the prevalence of fog at UK airfields.

The 121 was to be the world's first trijet airliner, and it was very close in design, looks and spec to the Boeing 727, but with the advantage

FIRST FACTS	
Launched	12/02/1958
First Flight	09/01/1962
Entered service	01/04/1964 BEA

STATS (1C)	
Length	34.98m (114ft 9in)
Height	8.23m (27ft)
Wingspan	27.38m 89(ft 10in)
Typical seats	103 max for 1C up to 180 max on 1E
Number built	117 across all versions

of being a good 12 months ahead. However, as mentioned, the BEA requirement was for a smaller, shorter-range aircraft and at the last minute the de Havilland company (soon to be Hawker Siddeley) agreed to the changes, which in hindsight killed off the greater international potential of the aircraft, handing what would probably be hundreds of orders to Boeing, who eventually

sold approximately 15 times more of the 727 than were sold of the Trident.

Consequently, the only orders for this very tailored version (Srs 1C) came from BEA – 24 airframes that were put into service from March 1964. However, BEA had by now realised their mistake and asked for a version with greater numbers all round. The Srs 1E was developed to appeal to the export market, having a greater payload/range, albeit within the same dimensions of the original. This succeeded in its intention, if only slightly, with Middle East carriers Kuwait Airways, Iraqi Airways and Pakistan International amongst the select few who ordered.

Despite being the driving force behind shrinking the aircraft in its initial design stage (and probably hurting sales versus the later 727), BEA rather quickly decided that they actually needed a longer-range version. Responding to this, Hawker

Siddeley produced the Srs 2E. However, this was not the success that was hoped for. In addition to BEA's 15, only two other customers ordered the new version, although CAAC's order for 33 did somewhat save face for the programme. Cyprus Airways ordered just two.

The final version for this rather missed opportunity of a programme was the Srs 3B, which had a fuselage stretch of 5m (16ft 5in) allowing up to 180 passengers. Interestingly, this aircraft actually had four engines – having limited power from the Spey engines, the 3B had a fourth placed in the tail section to add boost on take off.

Hawker Siddeley must have pondered on their decision-making over this project. The programme was well ahead of the Boeing 727 and surely would have won some of the 1,800 orders Boeing received had they made different choices sooner.

Lockheed Constellation

FIRST FACTS	-049	-749	-1049	-1649
Launched	1939	1947	N/A	05/55
Rolled out	N/A	N/A	N/A	10/10/56
Certification	N/A	03/47	11/51	N/A
First Delivery	07/43	18/04/47	15/12/51	05/57
Entered service	N/A	N/A	N/A	N/A
	USAAF	Air France	Eastern	TWA

Lockheed had been looking at a four-engined, pressurised airliner since 1937, but in 1939 Howard Hughes's TWA was in need of an airliner that could take 40 passengers over a range of 5,600km (3,500 miles). Lockheed responded with the L-049 Constellation. From the beginning the 'Connie', as it became known, was a design the likes of which had not been seen before. The fuselage was elegantly curved, almost dolphin like, thinning at the rear where it joined onto the easily recognisable triple tail arrangement, and all of this mounted on an undercarriage with rather long legs. This particularly beautiful lady was, however, diverted from a life of glamour into the US Army Air Force (USAAF) as a military transporter. It first flew on 9 January, 1943 and due to the outbreak of WW2 all orders were converted

into the military C-69 and bought by the military, although civilian airlines were contracted to fly the aircraft for the USAAF. The Connie suffered a chequered career in the military, having a number of technical issues centred around the Wright R-3350 engine, something that rather hampered the ongoing development of the aircraft.

At the end of the war the opposite happened to aircraft on the production line. Now not needed by the military, aircraft were finished to civilian specifications, with TWA receiving the first one on 1 October, 1945, putting it into service on 6 February, 1946.

The first of many new variants, the L-649, which flew for the first time on 19 October, 1946, was the first real civilian version of the aircraft but was overlooked by many airlines in favour of

the longer-range L-749, with Eastern being the only operator of note.

The L-749 was unveiled in early 1947 and was driven by the need for a longer-range aircraft, one that could cross the Atlantic Ocean non-stop. The aircraft first took to the air on 14 March, 1947 and after receiving certification the same month was delivered to launch customer Air France on 18 April, 1947. Despite problems at Lockheed, which stopped production at one point, the company went on to sell 119 aircraft to airlines such as Pan Am, Avianca, Cubana, KLM and TWA. The L-749 had another first when Pan Am used it to inaugurate the world's first around-the-world service.

The aircraft was continuously developed over the years until it gave way to the L-1049 Super Constellation, which first flew on 14 July, 1951. This version was even more successful than its predecessor, with nearly 260 aircraft flying mainly long-haul routes for airlines all around the globe. Lockheed had stretched this version by 5.59m (18ft 4in) allowing it to carry up to 95 passengers. In addition, 320 military versions were produced.

The last of the Constellation line was the L-1649 Starliner. Built in response to the long-range version of the DC7, it was in essence a Constellation with a new larger, high-aspect ratio wing. It first flew on 10 October, 1956 with TWA putting it into service in May 1957. However, time was not on the Starliner's side. Jets were coming over the horizon and only 44 were built, nearly all of them for TWA.

STATS	-049	-749	-1049	-1649
Length	29.03m (95ft 3in)	29.66m (97ft 4in)	34.62m (113ft 7in)	35.10m (116ft 2in)
Height	7.21m (23ft 8in)	6.83m (22t 5in)	7.54m (24ft 9in)	7.13m (23ft 4in)
Wingspan	37.49m (123ft)	37.49m (123ft)	37.62m (123ft 5in)	45.72m (150ft)
Typical/Max seats	43/60	60/81	69/95	71/92
No. built	88	119	265/320	43

McDonnell Douglas MD11

Developed from the DC10, the MD11 was updated, re-engined and stretched to seat up to 405 passengers. Launched in 1986, following orders for 52 aircraft from 12 airlines, the aircraft also sported a modified wing, becoming an early user of winglets. Initially, the aircraft failed to meet performance targets until subjected to a programme to reduce weight and drag.

Never a great seller, 200 of all versions were sold, with Finnair inaugurating passenger services in December 1990. American Airlines and Delta were big users of the passenger versions in the USA. Garuda, JAL, Varig, VASP, Swissair and KLM (who operated the last passenger service in October 2014) were also major users. Many aircraft remain in service today as freighters. Major operators include Lufthansa Cargo and by far the largest-ever operator FedEx, where they operate from their massive hub in Memphis.

It was initially thrown a lifeline in 1997 when Boeing stated that the aircraft would remain in production following their takeover of McDonnell Douglas; however, by the time June of 1998 arrived this decision was reversed and the very last aircraft was delivered in February 2000.

FIRST FACTS

Launched	30/12/86
First Delivery	29/11/90
Entered service	20/12/90 Finnair

STATS

Length	61.21m (200ft 10in)
Height	17.60m (57ft 9in)
Wingspan	51.66m (169ft 6in)
Typical/Max seats	248/285
Number built	200

Dornier 328JET

Fairchild Aerospace purchased an 80 per cent stake in Dornier in 1996 and soon after started development of the 328JET, which launched in 1997 with a number of regional operators placing orders for this turbofan-engined version of the Dornier 328 turboprop airliner.

The idea was hatched due to both a survey of regional airlines, which concluded that its passengers preferred pure jets over prop, as well as the expected operating economics. Added to this, the basic airframe of the 328 required only relatively minor modifications to take the jets.

The first 328JET was actually a conversion of the second 328 turboprop and made its first flight from Munich in Germany. The first delivery was to Skyways Airlines, with Hainan Airlines and Sun Air of Scandinavia also operating fleets. The aircraft was also marketed as a 34-passenger commuter aircraft or with an executive interior and named Envoy.

FIRST FACTS	
Launched	02/97
First Flight	20/01/98
Certification	06/99
First Delivery	Skyways Airlines

STATS	
Length	21.28m (69ft 10in)
Height	7.24m (23ft 9in)
Wingspan	20.98m (68ft 10in)
Range	1,656km (900nm/1035m)
Typical seats	34
Number built	83

Vickers Vanguard

Originally envisaged to be a next generation of turboprop airliner for British European Airlines (BEA), the Vanguard came a little late as it was by-passed with the arrival of pure jets and never got anywhere near its predecessor the Viscount. The design changed somewhat over the process from initial concept but ended up with seating for 126, using a double-bubble fuselage cross section and thereby creating plenty of belly hold space. The V.953 version could carry up to 139 passengers.

An initial order of 20 came from BEA, who were the main driver for the project, with TCA of Canada, who were coincidentally looking for a similar aircraft, ordering a total of 23. Other than the prototype, these were to be the only Vanguards produced, the majority of which were converted into Merchantmen freighters and found their way to carriers such as Air Bridge Carriers, Invicta International, Europe Aero Service and Hunting Cargo, with the latter still operating them into the second half of the 1990s.

FIRST FACTS

First Flight	20/01/56
First Delivery	12/60
Entered service	03/61 BEA

STATS

Length	37.45m (122ft 10 1/2in)
Height	10.64m (34ft 11in)
Wingspan	35.97m (118ft)
Typical seats	126
Number built	44

Beechcraft King Air

This popular business twin has had many different guises since it was first introduced to the public at the NBAA Convention in 1991. It has proved popular with not just the business community and private individuals, but with many of the world's armed forces. By April of 2013 more than 7,100 King Airs of all models had been delivered and were operating in 127 countries, having flown over 60 million hours.

The idea for the initial model 90 goes back as far as 1961, and since then well over 3,000 of these and the many subsequent versions have been sold to operators as diverse as Australia's Royal Flying Doctor Service to one used as a US Presidential aircraft.

FIRST FACTS

First Flight	20/01/64
Certification	11/08/80
First Delivery	07/07/64

STATS

Length	10.82m (35ft 6in)
Height	4.34m (14ft 3in)
Wingspan	15.32m (50ft 3in)
Max seats	7
Number built	3,100+

Convair CV990 Coronado

ROGER SYRATT

The CV990 was designed as an upgrade to the slow-selling CV880 and also to meet the needs of American Airlines, who required a transcontinental aircraft. The aircraft was beset with a number of problems during its flight-test phase, requiring modifications to reach its advertised speed and range guarantees. The two years it took to get the aircraft to meet these guarantees was unfortunately rather costly, not only in monetary terms but also in lost orders. Furthermore, Boeing responded with their 720 and later with the 727 which effectively killed off any chance of future orders.

On launch, American Airlines and Swissair did take their initial orders, as did Varig and Garuda, but these airlines were the only ones to operate the aircraft from new. These 37 aircraft did find their way into various other, mainly charter, operators via the second-hand market. The most notable was Spantax in Spain, who operated a total of 14 of the aircraft. The 990 does, however, still have a lasting legacy as it is still the fastest subsonic airliner ever built, flying at 990kmph, a speed that in part created the aircraft's designation.

FIRST FACTS	
Launched	07/58
First Flight	24/01/61
Entered service	03/62 American/Swissair

STATS	
Length	42.43m (139ft 2 1/2in)
Height	12.01m (39ft 5in)
Wingspan	36.58m (120ft)
Typical seats	149
Number built	37

Saab 340

Initially this programme was the first joint venture of its kind between European and US companies, with Saab working with Fairchild to produce what was conceived as a 'new generation' of turboprop. This collaboration created the initial designation of SF340.

Initial deliveries were to Crossair in Switzerland and Comair in the US (as 340As) and shortly afterwards, with the order book bulging, it became, at the time, the best-selling commuter aircraft in the world. However, in 1985 Fairchild decided that it no longer wanted to be in the aircraft manufacturing business, leaving Saab to continue on their own, and after that they dropped the 'SF' designation. The aircraft became popular with operators all over the globe. American Eagle became a major operator, with over 100 of the newest version – the 340B – which had more powerful engines and tailplane modifications leading to a better payload/range performance.

Unfortunately, even though the 340 was selling well, and even with a further enhancement (340B), Saab was actually losing money and in

FIRST FACTS	
Launched	09/80
First Flight	25/01/83
Certification	05/84
Entered service	06/84 Crossair

STATS	
Length	19.73m (64ft 9in)
Height	6.97m (22ft 11in)
Wingspan	21.44m (70ft 4in)
Typical/Max seats	30/36
Number built	458

1997 closed down production of both the 340 and 2000. A considerable number of aircraft are still in service today in commercial roles as well as in many of the specialist and military roles introduced over the years – roles such as Maritime Search and Rescue and Airborne early Warning and Control.

Boeing 737MAX

FIRST FACTS	MAX7	MAX8	MAX9
First Flight	16/03/18	29/01/16	13/04/17
Certification	N/A	09/03/17	00/02/18
First Delivery	N/A	06/05/17	21/03/18
Entered service	N/A	22/05/17	02/04/18
	N/A	Malindo Air	Thai Lion Air

Originally, Boeing had intended to replace the 737 series with a brand-new design, although this idea was ultimately shelved in favour of a re-engined version of the existing basic airframe. Airbus had launched its re-engined A320 in 2010 and very soon had over 1,000 orders. Amongst these was an order from American Airlines, who also wished to order the re-engined 737s from Boeing. This, in effect, forced Boeing's hand into producing what is now the MAX series.

Boeing's latest generation of its best-selling type had a number of changes over its predecessors, as you might expect. The range has more efficient CFM international LEAP 1B en-gines, airframe modifications, as well as split-tip winglets as standard, amongst other aero-dynamic improvements. Offered in four lengths, the MAX7, 8 and 9 replaced the 700, 800 and 900 srs respectively, and the further stretched MAX10 has also been added. The first to fly was the MAX8, and this aircraft first entered service with Malindo Air of Malaysia.

The decision to go with a re-engined version seems to have been a success as by the end of 2018 Boeing had received orders for over 4,300 aircraft. The decision also meant that a milestone was reached, with the 10,000th 737 delivered to long-time 737 user Southwest Airlines, a feat that has been recognised by Guinness World Re-

cords, who have awarded it the title of the most produced commercial jet aircraft model.

The MAX 9, which first flew on 13 April, 2017, entered service with launch customer Thai Lion Air in April 2018. The MAX 7 was next in the air on 16 March, 2018 and entry into service is expected in early 2019 with Southwest Airlines . The MAX 10 is still under construction with an expected entry into service date of 2020. As of the end of January 2019 there are 499 orders for this version.

STATS	MAX7	MAX8	MAX9
Length	35.56m (116ft 8in)	39.52m (129ft 8in)	42.26m (138ft 4in)
Height	12.30m (40ft 4in)	12.30m (40ft 4in)	12.30m (40ft 4in)
Wingspan	35.90m (117ft 10in)	35.90m (117ft 10in)	35.90m (117ft 10in)
Typical/Max seats	138/172	162/210	178/220
Number ordered	61	2,614	242

FEBRUARY

Boeing 747-8

Boeing had been thinking about a new variation of their iconic 747 from the early 90s and advertised it at the Farnborough Airshow in 1994. There was not, however, a great deal of interest shown in what would have been a -500/-600 series with a modified 777 wing. This idea was eventually shelved. Concerned about the A380 from Airbus, Boeing needed to produce something to take a segment of this expected market. They therefore continued to look at options for a future 747. The 747X was a stretched version of the then current model, which could carry up to 500 passengers. The 747-400XQLR (Quiet Long Range) was the next idea, which did not end in production either, but a lot of the ideas eventually ended up in the 747-8 via a programme called the 747 Advanced. The 747-8 also benefitted greatly from the 787 programme, with much of the technology developed for the Dreamliner being used in the 747-8.

This aircraft is 263ft longer than previous 747s and, in fact, it was the very first time in the history of the 747 programme that the fuselage had been lengthened.

The progress of this new 747 was not a smooth one. Slow orders and delays in pro-

FIRST FACTS	
First Flight	08/02/10 (747-8F)
Certification	19/08/11
First Delivery	12/10/11
	Cargolux

STATS	
Length	76.25m (250ft 2in)
Height	19.56m (64ft 2in)
Wingspan	68.4m (224ft 5in)
Typical/Max seats	410/467
Number ordered	156 (Jan 2019)

duction, in addition to a possible change in the world's aircraft needs, meant that by the end of January 2018 only 136 had been ordered, 65 per cent of which were the freight version, with no further Intercontinental passenger versions left on the books to add to the three airlines currently operating the aircraft. This version first flew on 11 March, 2011. The US government has also chosen this aircraft to be the next Presidential Aircraft as the VC-25B.

Boeing 727

FIRST FACTS	-100	-200
First Flight	09/02/63	27/07/67
Certification	24/12/63	30/11/67
First Delivery	29/10/63 United	14/12/67 Northeast
Entered service	01/02/64 Eastern	N/A N/A

Once the world's most produced jet airliner until its stable mate the 737 surpassed it, and the first to break the 1,000 sales barrier, the 727 was designed to service smaller airports with their often smaller runways. Boeing had only the 707/720 at that time, and with manufacturers all over the world planning and producing aircraft in this smaller sector, with aircraft such as the DC9, Caravelle, Trident and 1-11, Boeing needed to get in on this emerging market.

Boeing had struggled (and still were) with costs from the 707 programme and the risk of producing another brand-new type was one that many warned Boeing to avoid.

The brave decision to go ahead was mitigated by launch orders from United and Eastern of 40 aircraft each.

Although the aircraft retained the same cross section of the 707/720 fuselage, it had a number of firsts for Boeing. It was their first jetliner to undergo rigorous fatigue testing, the first to have completely powered flight controls, the first to use triple-slotted flaps and the first to have an auxiliary power unit (APU). APUs are commonplace now but were revolutionary in the mid-sixties, giving 727 operators the flexibility to operate from the more primitive airports of developing countries without the need for ground power or starting equipment.

An interesting fact is that the infamous DB Cooper hijacking took place on a Northwest Orient Airlines 727-100, assumedly chosen due to the rear steps allowing a relatively risk-free exit.

The 727 was over a year and a half behind the similarly configured HS Trident; however, this British-built aircraft was hampered by poor design changes pushed for by BEA. The 727 rolled out of the Renton plant on 27 November, 1962 in an interesting yellow/copper livery, and first flew on 9 February, 1963. The overall success of this type was not, however, initially apparent. Boeing had a break-even point of 200 airframes and the expectation of selling 250. But by the time of its first flight, sales were way short of these numbers.

In August of 1965 Boeing announced the 200 series, which subsequently first flew on 27 July, 1967. It was 6.1m (20ft) longer than the -100, which allowed up to 58 more passengers, although, as it had the same engines, it was at the cost of reduced range. The first customer, Northeast, introduced services that December.

The 727-200Advanced, with more powerful Pratt and Whitney JT8D engines, first flew on 3 March, 1972, entering service with All Nippon in July. The airframe had many variants over the years, with pure cargo and combi uses. In fact, many 727s are still in use today with cargo operators, but in quickly diminishing numbers.

When the Stage Three noise restrictions were being introduced, some operators tried to modify their aircraft to try and meet the new regulations. Hushkits and winglets as well as simple changes to flap and slat schedules were introduced, which remain on those aircraft still in service today.

These 200 series versions completely transformed the success of the type, with the last of 1,832 airframes delivered to FedEx in September 1984, ending a production run of 22 years. This aircraft is in service today with T2 Aviation as G-OSRA, an oil spill response aircraft.

The very first 727 to fly has been painstakingly renovated and made its very last flight on 2 March, 2016, ironically the exact opposite of the inaugural flight, this time from Paine Field to Boeing Field International, to take up residence at the adjacent Museum of Flight.

STATS	-100	-200
Length	40.59m (133ft 2in)	46.69m (153ft 2in)
Height	10.44m (34ft 3in)	10.44m (34ft 3in)
Wingspan	32.92m (108ft)	32.92m (108ft)
Typical/Max seats	114/131	145/189
Number built	572	1,260

Boeing 737NG Next Generation

FIRST FACTS	-600	-700	-800	-900
Announced	N/A	17/11/93	N/A	N/A
Launched	15/03/95	17/11/93	05/09/94	10/11/97
Rolled out	08/12/97	08/12/96	30/06/97	23/07/00
First Flight	22/01/98	09/02/97	31/07/97	03/08/00
Certification	18/08/98	07/11/97	13/03/98	17/04/01
First Delivery	18/09/98	17/12/97	22/04/98	16/05/01
Entered service	25/10/98 SAS	18/01/96 Southwest	24/04/98 Hapag-Lloyd	27/05/01 Alaska A/L

The Boeing 737-700 was the first of what was the third generation of 737s, alongside the -600/800 and 900. Originally designated 737X, this 'Next Generation' of 737s stretches back to 1991 when Boeing went out into the marketplace asking over 30 airlines what they needed from a new series of the popular twin jet. It was clearly a good plan as this generation brought in order after order.

Powered by CFM56-7 turbofans, which have greater efficiency than previous models, coupled with larger wings, thereby holding more fuel, provided greater range, which was significant for a US manufacturer as transcontinental USA flights were now possible.

The -700 was equivalent to the 'Classic' 300, with the -600 the 'Classic' 500 equivalent, the -800 was the -400 replacement and the -900 was a new stretched version aimed at competing with the Airbus A321. The programme was launched on 17 November, 1993 with an order for 63 plus a further 63 options from long-standing 737 operator Southwest. Even though 32 of those ordered were converted -300 options, it was still significant.

Just over three years later the first 737-700 rolled off the production line, taking to the skies on 9 February the following year. Certification followed nine months later. In total, the flight-test programme used 10 aircraft, four -700s, three -600s (first flight 22 January, 1998) and three -800s (first flight 31 July, 1997).

The 737 continued to make records with the 100 million miles flown mark passed in 2000,

the 1,000th Next Generation delivered (again to Southwest), and the 6,000th airframe (all marques) delivered to ILFC (Op by Norwegian) in 2009. The 8,000th was handed over to United Airlines in 2014, also meaning more than 4,000 of this generation alone had been delivered. This aircraft, the -900, was in fact the final version to fly on 3 August, 2000, and it had benefitted from a number of enhancements over the original. These enhancements also found their way into the other marques. The -900 found a particularly good home in the US with majors like United, Delta and Alaska purchasing large numbers, although selling well around the rest of the world as well. The best-selling of all the marques, however, is the -800, which sold over 5,000, similar in total to all of the other Next Generation, Classic and Original versions combined

STATS	-600	-700	-800	-900
Length	31.24m (102ft 6in)	33.60m (110ft 4in)	39.47m (129ft 6in)	33.88m (111ft 2in)
Height	12.57m (41ft 3in)	12.57m (41ft 3in	12.55m (41ft 2in)	12.55m (41ft 2in)
Wingspan	34.31m (112ft 7in)	34.31m (112ft 7in)	34.31m (112ft 7in)	34.31m (112ft 7in)
Typical/Max seats	108/132	126/149	162/189	177/189
No. ordered (03/18)	69	1,164	5,151	562

Boeing 747-100/200

FIRST FACTS	-100	-200
First Flight	09/02/69	11/10/70
Certification	12/69	N/A
First Delivery	15/01/70	16/01/71
	Pan Am	KLM

The iconic Boeing 747 was nothing short of revolutionary when it first came on the scene at the end of the 1960s. The combination of huge passenger numbers and more efficient high bypass engines brought air travel to a whole new market as airlines could now offer much cheaper fares than before. This once 'must have' aircraft, however, very nearly broke the Boeing company. The Queen of the Skies could so easily have remained firmly on the ground.

Back in 1963, Boeing were in competition with other manufacturers for a new large military transport aircraft. Boeing were not successful in their bid, the winners being Lockheed with General Electric, whose design went on to become the C5 Galaxy. However, it was a time of rapid growth in the commercial aviation world and in that world were some larg-er-than-life characters, arguably the largest of these being a big Boeing customer, Juan Trippe of Pan Am.

Trippe was looking for an aircraft that would double the current capacity offered by the 707 and DC8. Airports were becoming congested and Trippe saw an aircraft of this size solving the problem by moving more people in one go. Trippe obviously had both vision and the ability to push through his ideas as he was involved in all phases of the design and development for the aircraft, and not surprisingly Pan Am became the launch customer with an order for 25.

The project did have to overcome some significant turbulence: first and foremost the incredibly short timescale of just 28 months from design to delivery, the need to build a whole new construction facility, which is still the largest building in the world by volume today, and difficulties with overheating engines and meeting evacuation times. These challenges led to another potentially more critical one, the small matter of a $2billion debt, a figure that would equate to something like $12 billion today. However, the storm was weathered and the 747 took to the skies on 9 February, 1969, and the order book at the time was at a healthy 160 from an equally healthy 27 airlines.

Pan Am inaugurated services on the New York to London route less than a year later on 22 January, 1970, ushering in a new era of air travel.

Boeing had always envisaged more powerful versions of the 747 and the first of these were grouped together under the 747-200 – 200B for passenger, 200C for convertible, 200M for Combi and 200F for freighter – the latter featuring an upwardly hinging door, thus enabling the easy loading of the 29 standard pallets or containers it was capable of carrying on its main deck in addition to the 'standard' cargo hold which takes up to 30 ULD containers. The combo version also had a large cargo door at the rear of the port fuselage, which allowed the carriage of both passengers and freight together. The first 747-200, a 'B' passenger version, first flew on 11 October, 1970, with KLM taking the first of these on 16 January, 1971.

The 747-100/200 has had some interesting variations. NASA acquired two -100s, which were converted for use as Space Shuttle transports to take the Orbiters back from the landing site to the Kennedy space centre. The US Air Force used four as E-4 Advanced Airborne Command Posts. However, arguably the most well-known are the VC25A VIP aircraft, better known as Air Force One, although this term is actually the official air traffic control call sign for any USAF aircraft with the president on board, not the aircraft itself.

STATS	-100	-200
Length	70.66m (231ft 10in)	70.66m (231ft 10in)
Height	19.33m (63ft 5in)	19.33m (63ft 5in)
Wingspan	59.64m (195ft 8in)	59.64m (195ft 8in)
Typical/Max seats	366/442	366/452
Number Built	205	389

Douglas DC4/C-54

The aircraft we know as the DC4 is actually the second design to bear this designation. Originally a pressurised 52-seater, it soon became clear, despite input from several major airlines, that it was too big and expensive, so Douglas changed the design to a 44-seater unpressurised airframe, which was much more an aircraft for the time. Powered by four Pratt & Whitney R-2000 Twin Wasps, it was aimed at medium- to long-range routes, and at a much lower purchase price and operating costs, the DC4A as it was now termed had attracted over 60 orders by the time of its first flight on 14 February, 1942.

However, its entry into commercial service was delayed by the Japanese attack on Pearl Harbour just two months prior to this first flight. All the aircraft destined for commercial operators were diverted to the US military as C-54 (USAAF) and R5D (Navy). It wasn't until 1945 that civilian operators started to acquire them, the majority of which were civilianised C-54s, although a few DC4s were produced following the end of the war. These aircraft served with the likes of Sabena, KLM, Northwest, Swissair, Trans Australia and Western.

FIRST FACTS	
First Flight	14/02/42
First Delivery	02/43
	USAAF

STATS	
Length	28.63m (93ft 11in)
Height	8.38m (27ft 6in)
Wingspan	35.81m (117ft 6in)
Number built	1243
Typical/Max seats	44/86

Of the 1,243 built (of all variants), just a small number remain in service, with Buffalo Airways of Ice Pilots fame being possibly the largest operator and a few others preserved and flying on the airshow circuit.

An interesting variant was the Aviation Traders Carvair which, based on the DC4/C54, carried 22 passengers in the rear cabin with five cars in the front. This aircraft first flew on 21 June, 1961. A total of just 21 were built.

Douglas DC6

FIRST FACTS	DC6	DC6A/B
First Flight	15/02/46	29/09/49
First Delivery	24/11/46 United/American	03/51 Slick Airways

Despite the availability of cheap C-54/DC4 aircraft after WW2, many of the US majors wanted a bigger and faster version of this aircraft. Lockheed were offering the Constellation, so Douglas produced an upgraded DC4 in the shape of the DC6. This aircraft was 2.03m (6ft 8in) longer with a pressurised cabin and square windows, but it was a lot more than just that. Many commercial aviation firsts were introduced on the DC6, such as reversible props, cargo containers that could be pre-loaded, air conditioning whilst on the ground and provision was made for the installation of weather radar, to name a few.

The initial design came from a USAAF project towards the end of WW2; however, the prototype (named XC-112) arrived too late, as by the time of the first flight on 15 February, 1946 the war had, of course, ended. The design was modified to the requirements of the US majors and the civil DC6 first flew on 29 June, 1946. Initial deliveries were made in the November, with United inaugurating trans-

continental service in April the following year. The aircraft took substantially less time to go coast to coast than its smaller sibling, but more importantly around an hour quicker than the competing Constellation. Despite an early problem with fires in the fuselage that grounded the fleet for four months, orders kept coming. Pan Am, Delta, Braniff, Mexicana and Aerolineas Argentinas being some examples.

Douglas further developed the aircraft, with the slightly longer DC6A first flying on 29 September, 1949. This version was aimed at the cargo market, with loading doors and a strengthened floor. The DC6B was the upgraded passenger version, first flown on 2 February, 1951. United took delivery of the first of the type in April of 1951. This version opened up a whole new set of routings with (eastbound) non-stop transatlantic crossings now possible.

There are still quite a number of DC6s around the world being used as freighters and fire-fighting aircraft as well as the odd ground-based restaurant!

STATS	DC6	DC6A/B
Length	30.66m (100ft 7in)	32.18m (105ft 7in)
Height	8.66m (28ft 5in)	8.66m (28ft 5in)
Wingspan	35.81m (117ft 6in)	35.81m (117ft 6in)
Typical/Max seats	74/84	82/102
Number Built	704 of all variants	

Boeing 757

FIRST FACTS	757-200	757-300
Launched	13/08/78	09/96
First Flight	19/02/82	03/08/98
Certification	21/12/82	N/A
Entered service	01/01/83 Eastern	03/99 Condor Flugdienst

In the 1970s Boeing were looking at options to replace the extremely popular 727, and in 1978, after various proposals, announced what was then called the 7N7. Using the tried and tested fuselage cross section from the 707/727/737 fleets, they added a new nose and wings as well as incorporating an EFIS flight deck. In addition, there was a high bypass turbofan under each wing.

This is significant because it was the first time Boeing had offered an aircraft with an engine from a foreign manufacturer, in this case Rolls Royce, with the RB535C. The programme was launched with orders from British Airways and Eastern Airlines and the first flight took place on 19 Febru-

ary, 1982, the aircraft by then being designated 757-200. Eastern were the first to put this aircraft, with its new technology, in to service on 1 January, 1983. The aircraft was granted extend-

ed range operations (EROPS) in December 1986, this being the start of the many 757 transatlantic and intercontinental services we see today. In the initial years, Boeing offered just two options on the base model: the 757-200PF, which was very much aimed at the small package operators, with UPS ordering 59 and FedEx and DHL following with orders of their own later, and a combo version, the 200M, was also produced, but this was not taken up in any great numbers.

By the time the 757-300 was introduced, orders had come in from all parts of the globe.

Launched in September of 1996, the 757-300 first flew on 3 August, 1998. The fuselage was over seven metres longer than the -200 and aimed squarely at the European inclusive tour market, often carrying 289 passengers in a high-density layout. The first delivery was made to Condor in March 1999.

The 757 sold 1,049 in all to 54 customers and found homes not only with the world's airlines but also with the military, VIP carriers, as private jets and as research aircraft, such was its versatility.

STATS	757-200	757-300
Length	47.32m (155ft 3in)	54.43m (178ft 7in)
Height	13.56m (44ft 6in)	13.56m (44ft 6in)
Wingspan	38.05m (124ft 10in)	38.05m (124ft 10in)
Typical/Max seats	178/231	243/289
Number Built	994	55

Embraer 170/190

FIRST FACTS	170	175	190	195
First Flight	19/02/02	14/06/03	12/03/04	07/12/04
Certification	19/02/04	23/12/04	30/12/05	30/06/06
First Delivery	08/03/04	N/A	N/A	N/A
Entered service	N/A	07/05	N/A	N/A
	LOT	Air Canada	Jet Blue	N/A

The 170 was the first to fly from the then new range of jet aircraft following on from the ERJ135/145. Announced in February 1999, Embraer had been looking at options for a 70-seat aircraft for some time, initially based around the existing nose and cockpit of the ERJ family with a new fuselage and wing. However, by the time of the announcement the decision was made to produce a family that eventually consisted of the 170/175/190/195, all of which were to be a completely new design. Crossair and Regional were the launch customers with orders for both the 170 and 190; however, it was LOT Polish airlines who received the first aircraft on 8 March, 2004.

The aircraft performs well in both hot and high destinations, as well as those with short runways. All the aircraft are also licensed to fly into London City airport using the 5.5 degree approach. The slightly stretched 175 flew for the first time in June 2003, with the much larger 190 making its first flight on 12 March, 2004, with the 195 just short of eight months later on 7 December. The family of aircraft has garnered orders from all around the globe, with major users being JetBlue, Republic and Skywest Airlines in the US and Azul back home in Brazil.

STATS	170	175	190	195
Length	29.90m (98ft 1in)	31.68m (103ft 11in)	32.64m (118ft 11in)	38.65m (126ft 10in)
Height	9.64m (31ft 7in)	9.64m (31ft 7in)	10.39m (34ft 1in)	10.37m (34ft)
Wingspan	26.00m (85ft 3in)	26.00m (85ft 3in)	28.72m (94ft 3in)	28.72m (94ft 3in)
Typical/Max seats	70/80	76/88	96/114	100/124
No. ordered (10/18)	191	647	563	172

Airbus A320ceo

FIRST FACTS	318	319	320	321
Announced	07/09/98	N/A	N/A	N/A
Launched	26/04/99	10/06/93	23/03/84	24/11/88
Rolled out	N/A	24/08/95	14/02/87	03/03/93
First Flight	15/01/02	29/08/95	22/02/87	11/03/93
Certification	23/05/03	10/04/96	26/02/88	17/12/93
First Delivery	22/07/03	25/04/96	28/03/88	27/01/94
Entered service	N/A	08/05/96	N/A	18/03/94
	Frontier A/L	Swissair	Air France	Lufthansa

The A320 was the first of a new family of single-aisle aircraft produced by Airbus following on from the success of the A300 programme, designed to compete with the 737 and DC9, which were dominating the short-haul market at the time.

A wider fuselage cross section was adopted by Airbus, enabling a wider cabin and therefore providing greater comfort for the passengers; however, probably the most notable innovation was the use of fly-by-wire controls. This process sends electrical signals to the control surfaces telling them what to do, rather than the traditional mechanical pro-cess. This meant that the control yoke, which had previously sat directly in front of the flight crew for pretty much the whole history of flight, was no longer necessary, and Airbus replaced it with what they termed a 'sidestick' which was, and still is, essentially a joystick similar to that used by flight sim enthusiasts. The benefits of such a design are that it provides protection of the flight envelope by making it almost impossible to fly beyond certain flight parameters, such as 'g' forces, max speed and angle of attack and possibly most importantly it would not allow the aircraft to enter a stall.

European manufacturers both individually and collaboratively had been looking at an aircraft to compete with the dominant US manufacturers since the early 1970s, and in June 1977 a new programme called Joint European Transport (JET) was set up by members of the Airbus programme, but interestingly not as an official Airbus project initially. Considered as the forerunner to the A320 programme, it was in fact transferred to Airbus, who then took it on to look at three possibilities for the A320 but which ironically would all come to fruition in the future as the variants we know today, namely the A319 and A321.

By the time the 1980s arrived, the project was officially called A320 with the initial version being the -100, although very few were actually built of this version as the -200 was able to carry considerably more fuel, therefore flying further, with the introduction of a centre fuel tank and winglets. To keep weight, and therefore operating costs, as low as possible, particularly important with the oil price rises of the 1970s, the aircraft was designed with a two-crew cockpit and good degree of composite materials as well as the most up-to-date and fuel-efficient turbofan engines.

As with previous Airbus aircraft, production was spilt between partner companies around Europe; however, government interference, most notably in the UK, stalled the project for around three years.

On 23 March, 1984 the programme was officially launched. The order book was already totalling just short of 100 aircraft, with Air France being the first. Orders steadily increased, with a significant order of 100 from US airline Northwest coming just a few months before the first flight on 22 February, 1987, after a celebratory roll out just eight days earlier. Certification came almost exactly a year later, leading to launch customer Air France receiving their first aircraft on 28 March, 1988.

As with all Airbus aircraft, the different main sections are constructed around Europe, with the forward fuselage being from Saint Nazaire in France, the wings from Broughton in the UK, and the rear fuselage from Hamburg and vertical tail plane (VTP) from Stade in Germany. (In fact, every single VTP for every single Airbus ever constructed was made at Stade.) All are then brought by Beluga to the final assembly line (FAL) in Toulouse, France.

The first derivative of the programme, the A321-100, was launched on 24 November, 1989, with the first flight being made on 11 March, 1993. There were limited changes made to the A321 other than the stretch of 6.93m (22ft 9in). The undercarriage was strengthened to make up for the extra weight of the two fuselage plugs either side of the wing, with refinements made to the fuel system and larger tyres. The wing was slightly modified so that the aircraft handling characteristics were close to the A320, which helped pilots who flew A320/321s and 319s as the three types shared a common type rating because the cockpits were identical.

Initial delivery was made to Lufthansa on 27 January, 1994 with the airline putting it into service on 18 March. A little short on range, Airbus launched the A321-200 version in April 1995. This version had the range to make transcontinental USA routes non-stop with a full passenger load, again mainly by adding a centre fuel tank. This version first flew on 12 December, 1996 and was first operated by the now defunct Monarch Airways on 24 April, 1997

The next version offered was the smaller A319, which is seven frames or 3.73m (12ft 3in) shorter than the A320. It was launched on 10 June, 1993 making its first flight on 29 August, 1995 from Hamburg Finkenwerder. At the time of launch only six aircraft were ordered, and although ordered by Air Inter these actually went to Air France as the two carriers merged. Further orders soon followed, and from many of the European and US majors, with Swissair being the first of these to put it into service on 8 May, 1996.

Airbus also launched a shortened version of the A319, the A318, on 26 April, 1999, with a healthy order book of 109 orders and options. However, there were no further orders and after cancellations this figure went down to 80, which is where it has stayed ever since. Frontier airlines accepted the first A318 on 22 July, 2003, it is also used by the likes of Avianca, Air France and TAROM. A number of orders for this jet were for the ACJ318 Elite, the corporate jet version which was offered in conjunction with Lufthansa Technic.

The A318 has also been certified for a 5.5 degree approach and is the largest airliner to have been so, which led to British Airways ordering it to operate its BA001 flight, which moved to London City after the withdrawal of its Concorde fleet in 2003.

As of the end of August 2018, orders for each variant, which now have the suffix ceo for current engine option with the introduction of neo or new engine option for each of the variants, is as follows: A318 80, A319ceo 1489, A320ceo 4770, A321ceo 1800.

Such has been the success of this family of aircraft that final assembly has had to be spread out across not only Europe but the world. Toulouse now only has an A320 Final Assembly line (FAL) with Hamburg taking on the assembly of the A321 and A319 in addition to its own A320 FAL. Furthermore, in Tianjin, China, there is now an A319 and A320 FAL and over to the west in Mobile, Alabama in the USA there are FALs for the A319/320/321.

STATS	318	319	320	321
Length	31.45m (103ft 2in)	33.83m (111ft)	37.57m (123ft 3in)	44.51m (146ft)
Height	12.51m (41ft)	11.76m (38ft 7in)	11.76m (38ft 7in)	11.76m (38ft 7in)
Wingspan	35.80m (117ft 5in)	35.80m (117ft 5in)	35.80m (117ft 5in)	35.80m (117ft 5in)
Typical/Max seats	117/136	124/156	152/180	185/220
No. ordered (08/18)	80	1489	4770	1800

Boeing 737 Classic

FIRST FACTS	-300	-400	-500
First Flight	24/02/84	19/02/88	20/06/89
Certification	14/11/84	02/09/88	12/02/90
First Delivery	28/11/84	15/09/88	28/02/90
Entered service	N/A	N/A	N/A
	US Air	Piedmont	Southwest

Boeing's 737 had its first make over with the introduction of the 737-300, the first of what is now called the classic series, the others being the -400 and -500. This second generation of the hugely popular airframe was driven by the need to improve range and increase capacity (The -300 was 2.64m or 8ft 6in longer than the -200.) The major leap forward was the use of the much quieter and more fuel efficient CFM56 turbofan engines.

However, Boeing had to overcome some issues with mating the engine to the wing given the low ground clearance the 737 has. To overcome the challenge, Boeing decided to mount the engine not directly under the wing but somewhat forward of it, as well as 'flattening' the underside of the nacelle, giving it a rather unique looking profile. In addition, an EFIS flight deck was introduced, there was an increase in the use of composite materials and a number of aerodynamic improvements to the wing. The 737-300 first flew on 24 February, 1984, having rolled out of Renton on 17 January, and it was particularly popular from the outset, account-

ing for well over half of the nearly 2,000 aircraft from the classic series combined, with launch customer Southwest alone operating 150.

The -400 was the next to fly nearly four years later on 19 February, 1988, with Piedmont being the first to place this further stretched and higher-weight version into service, although it also found a small niche as a high-density aircraft for IT companies.

The last classic to fly was the shorter -500, which was in fact the closest in size to the -200, and therefore a direct replacement. It first flew on 20 June, 1989 with Southwest yet again being the launch customer. Boeing surpassed its own record of most commercial jet airliners ever produced (held by the 727) in early 1990 with the delivery of the 1,833rd 737, a 300 series operated by British Midland.

STATS	-300	-400	-500
Length	33.40m (109ft 7in)	36.45m (119ft 7in)	31.01m (101ft 9in)
Height	11.13m (36ft 6in)	11.13m (36ft 6in)	11.13m (36ft 6in)
Wingspan	28.88m (94ft 9in)	28.88m (94ft 9in)	28.88m (94ft 9in)
Typical/Max seats	128/149	146/172	108/132
No. built	1113	486	389

Douglas DC9

FIRST FACTS	-10	-30	-40	-50
First Flight	25/02/65	01/08/66	28/11/67	17/12/74
Certification	23/11/65	N/A	02/68	N/A
First Delivery	N/A	N/A	N/A	08/75
Entered service	08/12/65	1967	03/68	N/A
	Delta A/L	Eastern	SAS	Swissair

Needing to add a short to medium-range airliner to complement the DC8, Douglas's initial design for a smaller aircraft did not create enough interest from airlines and was cancelled in favour of a marketing agreement with Sud Aviation for its Caravelle. Similarly unsuccessful, Douglas went back to the drawing board in 1962 and came up with a T-tailed, twin rear-mounted engine aircraft with built in airstairs both at the front and in the tail aimed at short hops, often into airports with shorter runways and little infrastructure. Delta Airlines at this time was also looking for a replacement for its ageing CV440s. It was indeed Delta who was the launch customer for the aircraft with an order of 15 placed in April 1963. The first flight was on 25 February, 1965, but with orders for just over 50 there were concerns for the longevity of the programme.

Douglas persevered with the design, producing what was to become the best-selling version, the -30. This larger version, which first flew on 1 August, 1966, carried more passengers, and had improved wings, engines and greater fuel capacity. Eastern were the first to put this version into service, doing so in Febru-

ary 1967. This version went on to sell 662, well over half the total number of DC9s ever built.

Not so popular versions were the -20 – especially useful for short landing fields and first flown on 18 September, 1968 – and the -15 – a longer range version of the -10.

The -40 was the next to come and it was a further 1.8m (6ft) longer than the -30, taking to the skies on 28 November, 1967, with SAS putting the aircraft into service in March the following year.

The final variant, the -50, was the largest of this initial version of the DC9 with another stretch of 2.44m (8ft), thereby enabling it to carry up to 139 passengers, propelled by its more powerful JT8D engines. First taking to the skies on December 17, 1974, it garnered orders from the likes of Swissair, Eastern, Allegheny and Finnair.

STATS	-10	-30	-40	-50
Length	31.82m (104ft 5in)	36.36m (113ft 9in)	38.28m (125ft 7in)	40.72m (133ft 7in)
Height	8.38m (27ft 6in)	8.38m (27ft 6in)	8.53m (28ft)	8.53m (28ft)
Wingspan	27.25m (89ft 5in)	28.47m (93ft 5in)	28.47m (93ft 5in)	28.47m (93ft 5in)
Typical/Max seats	80/90	105/115	N/A/125	N/A/139
No. built	137	621	71	96

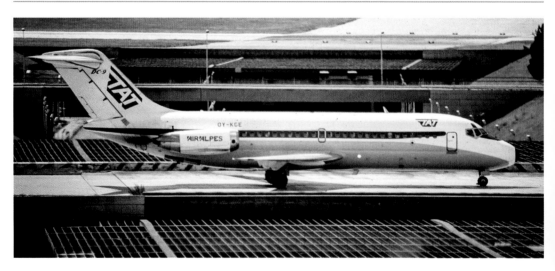

Antonov AN22 Antheus

This four-engine, heavy transport aircraft, with the unfortunate NATO reporting name of 'Cock', is the largest turboprop in the world. Easily identifiable, it sports contra rotating props and a twin-tail layout, as well making a distinctive engine noise. It was also the Soviet's first wide-body aircraft. Originally designed as a strategic airlifter for the Soviet Union, it can deliver its 229 passengers or 80,000kg (176,350lb) of freight on an unpressurised deck (it had a pressurised cabin able to hold 29 passengers just aft of the cockpit) to a range of 5,000km (3,100 miles). It first flew on 27 February, 1965, with production being terminated early in 1975 after just 68 were built. As with many Soviet aircraft, the AN22 was designed for rough field operations, with pilots having the ability to change the pressure of each of its 24 tyres to suit different airstrips. Very few remain airworthy today; however, Antonov Airlines operates one commercially from its base at Gostomel near Kiev.

FIRST FACTS

Launched	1962
Rolled out	18/08/64
First Flight	27/02/65
First Delivery	1969 Soviet Air Transport Wing

STATS

Length	57.92m (211ft 4in)
Height	57.91m (190ft)
Wingspan	64.40m (211ft 4in)
Payload	229 pax or 80,000kg
Number built	68

MARCH

BAC/Aérospatiale Concorde

Possibly the best-known commercial airliner ever built, Concorde was an anglo-french built supersonic passenger airliner and the only one to ever really enter commercial service. An aviation work of art, this aircraft made supersonic travel routine, transporting passengers across the Atlantic so fast that arrival in New York was actually earlier than the departure time in Europe. It could be said that transition to supersonic speed was actually an anti-climax as the only way passengers were aware they had reached the speed of sound was the Mach-meter on the forward bulkhead. If you were lucky enough to make it into the cockpit you might also be shown that the aircraft had in fact stretched in flight – although reports vary as to the amount, it was somewhere between five and twelve inches.

The aircraft had to overcome many challenges to both get into the air and stay there but ultimately failed to do so, although not in terms of its engineering achievements or its importance to aviation, but because it never fully reached its undoubted potential, a magnificent creature that there were never enough of and that left the skies before its time.

Initially, both Sud Aviation in France and the Bristol Aircraft company, who had joined together, found that they had actually designed similar concepts, with the only disagreements being over the size and range of the aircraft. The further difficulties of navigating through the very murky waters of international politics were ironically made easier by the UK's wish to join the European Common Market. An international draft treaty was signed in November 1962. Even whether to include the 'e' at the end of its name created political uproar.

FIRST FACTS	
Launched	29/11/62
Rolled out	12/65
First Flight	02/03/69
Certification	10/75
Entered service	21/01/76 BA Air France

The cost of the programme was yet another hurdle to get over – the initial budget of around £70 million had, by the time of the draft agreement, reached £150 million. Two years later it had doubled to £300 million. By the end of the programme the final cost had been estimated at anything from £1.3 to £2.1 billion.

However, these initial challenges were overcome and, following the start of construction in February 1965, Concorde 001 took to French skies in Toulouse on 2 March, 1969, the present home of Airbus. As the aircraft were being assembled in both France and the UK, the next to take to the air was on 9 April of the same year from the runway at Bristol Filton. The aircraft first went supersonic on 1 October. Both of these aircraft differed slightly from the production versions but had the variable geometry drooping nose which was lowered for taxi, take off and landing to enable the pilots to actually see where they were going, but was raised in flight, as well as the slender delta wing to create the ultra-aerodynamic and beautiful shape in the cruise.

Unfortunately, the problems kept on coming. Initial forecasts of sales were for something in the region of 350, with around 100 options reserved by airlines around the world. Then 1973 arrived. A combination of the stock market crash, the actual crash of the Soviet TU144 and the oil crisis in that year, alongside the growing issue of countries not allowing supersonic overfly rights other than over water and the spiralling costs, scared the majority of customers away. British Airways and Air France were eventually the only airlines to operate Concorde.

Being designed for transatlantic operations, both the British and French airlines intended to use the aircraft on routes from Europe to the USA. However, a ban by the US congress on Concorde operations due to perceived noise levels initially delayed these services. Once operating, it was later found that the US Presidential aircraft at the time was actually noisier than Concorde when flying at subsonic speeds during take off and landing, effectively ending the noise debate.

Still owned by the governments and not the airlines, the aircraft were losing money year after year, there were accusations of government subsidies and the continued future was in doubt. In the UK, BA persuaded the government to sell the aircraft for a reported £16.5 million plus the first year's profits. Combined with an increase in the fares, Concorde had now become operationally profitable. Another source of income and one that also enabled Concorde enthusiasts all over the world to sample flying at twice the speed of sound were regular charters of both BA and Air France aircraft to European destinations, sporting events and even circular trips.

Unfortunately for Concorde, this period of profitability and security was all about to change. 25 July, 2000 saw the lowest point in the life of Concorde. AF 4590, a charter flight from Paris to New York, ran through debris during the take-off run. This debris caused the tyre to fail, subsequently rupturing a fuel tank. The ensuing fire led to a loss of control, with the aircraft crashing shortly after killing all on board, as well as four people on the ground. Later that year the 11 September attacks had a serious effect on passenger numbers throughout the aviation industry.

Despite modifications to the aircraft to ensure an event like the Paris crash could never happen again, both BA and Air France made simultaneous announcements on 10 April, 2003 that both their fleets would be retired later that year. Virgin Atlantic offered to buy the BA fleet but this was dismissed; however, this is probably a moot point as Airbus had also stated that it was no longer going to provide support for continued maintenance.

After a round of farewell flights, most of the remaining examples were flown to new homes in museums around the world. The very last flight by Concorde was on 26 November, 2003, with a BA aircraft flying to Bristol from London Heathrow.

STATS	
Length	61.66m (202ft 4in)
Height	12.20m (40ft 2in)
Wingspan	25.6m (83ft 10in)
Typical/Max seats	100/128
Number built	20

Yakovlev YAK42

Designed to replace the TU134 as well as the AN24/26 and IL18 turboprops, its roots go back to the early 70s. The aircraft was to be used on Soviet domestic routes, often into airfields with limited support equipment. Yakovlev were unsure just what the configuration should be so manufactured three different prototypes, the first two having different wing sweeps. The first prototype, which had an 11-degree sweep, first flew on 7 March, 1975. The second had a 23-degree sweep and had done away with storage for coats and carry-on baggage, which consequently provided 20 more seats. The production standard turned out to be based on the third prototype, which was a slightly modified version of the second.

Mainly ordered by Aeroflot, the three-engined aircraft, which by now had gained the NATO name of 'Clobber', was first put into service on their Moscow-Krasnodar route, with other aircraft going to Cuba and China. In later years and following the break-up of the Soviet Union, the YAK 42 found itself in many different liveries with a number still in operation today.

There were a number of variants created with enhanced avionics and greater range as well as a number of specialist uses. There were further projected versions, none of which flew but the basis of which ended up being incorporated in the design of the Irkut MC-21.

FIRST FACTS

First Flight	07/03/75
Entered service	22/12/80 Aeroflot

STATS

Length	34.88m (114ft 5in)
Height	9.83m (32ft 3in)
Wingspan	25.6m (83ft 10in)
Typical seats	104/120
Number built	185

Ilyushin IL76

The IL76 (Candid) came about from a need to transport 40 tonnes of freight over 5,000km (3100 miles) in under six hours, often into short and unprepared airstrips in difficult weather, particularly in icy Siberia. The design, with a high wing, T-tail and podded engines to minimise possible damage, was dictated from needs these airfields produced. Its rear loading ramp meant that it could carry large specific items as well as provide quick and relatively safe egress for paratroops. It was intended to be a direct replacement for the AN12, which had been in service with Soviet Military Transport Aviation since 1959 as its standard medium-range paratroop and cargo transport, as well as with other operators in civilian roles.

It was first thought about in the late 1960s but it didn't fly until 25 March, 1971. Initially two variants were produced: the IL76M for the military with added defensive capabilities and the IL76T, which was aimed at civilian use and, with the reduction in weight due to the lack of armaments, could carry more fuel and subsequently fly further with a greater payload.

The first deliveries were to the Soviet Airforce in 1974, with Aeroflot receiving their first

FIRST FACTS	
First Flight	25/03/71
First Delivery	06/74 Soviet Airforce

STATS	
Length	46.59m (152ft 10in)
Height	14.76m (48ft 5in)
Wingspan	50.50m (165ft 8in)
Max payload	40,000kg (88,185lb)
Number built	960 approx

aircraft in 1976. The aircraft has had many different roles, including firefighting, medevac, search and rescue, Antarctic supply, Zero G training for Soviet cosmonauts, ECM and reconnaissance. The basis of the airframe has also been used to create the IL78 airborne refueller, the A50 AEW&C, and an airborne laser flying laboratory designated the A60.

A new version, the IL76MD-90A, is still in production and many of its predecessors are still flying in both civilian and military roles.

Curtiss C46

ROGER SYRATT

The C-46 Commando was originally designed as the CW-20, a 36-seat pressurised passenger airliner of all-metal construction. However, with the first flight being on 26 March, 1940 the world was already at war and the aircraft was evolved into a transport aircraft. The aircraft had a number of changes: gone was the pressurisation system, as was one of the original two tail fins. Brought in to enhance the design for its new role was a large cargo door, leading to a strengthened floor with the ability to carry personnel in addition to cargo on folding seats along the cabin walls.

The aircraft underwent a few further modifications throughout the war years but suffered from an abnormal number of inflight losses due to explosion. Ultimately this was traced to leaking gasoline pooling in the wings. This issue was fixed post-war with vents made in the wings. After the war, the aircraft did not make as much of an impact as its smaller companion the DC3 in the commercial market due to the larger size, but it was still operated by a considerable number of airlines, including Avianca, BOAC, Arkia, Alitalia, Pan Am and Delta Airlines. The aircraft is still active but in much fewer numbers than the original number of over 3,000 built, with possibly the most well-known being operated by Buffalo Airways in Canada's far north.

FIRST FACTS	
First Flight	26/03/40
Entered service	N/A
	US Army Air Corps

STATS	
Length	23.37m (76ft 4in)
Height	6.63m (21ft 9in)
Wingspan	32.94m (108ft)
Max payload	5275kg (11,630lb)
Typical/Max seats	40/62
Number built	3,341 approx

Saab 2000

With airlines moving towards creating regional operations using aircraft with greater capacity than previously, Saab decided to stretch its popular 340. The resulting 50-seat airliner could just about match block times of jets on these routes but with the economy of turboprops. The programme was launched with an order from Crossair, and subsequent orders from other airlines combined with options meant that the total was 192 by April 1991.

Externally, other than the stretch, the aircraft was very similar to the 340; however, it had a larger wing and six-bladed props, whilst internally advanced avionics and a noise suppression system had been added. The aircraft first flew on 26 March, 1992, with Crossair putting it into service in December of the following year. Despite the perceived operating economics, the 2000 did not sell well enough against its jet rivals, and after just 63 were built over a production run of just seven years Saab closed both the 2000 and 340 production lines.

FIRST FACTS

Launched	15/12/88
Rolled out	11/91
First Flight	26/03/92
Certification	03/94
First Delivery	N/A
Entered service	09/94 Crossair

STATS

Length	27.28m (89ft 6in)
Height	7.72m (25ft 4in)
Wingspan	24.76m (81ft 3in)
Typical/Max seats	50/58
Number built	63

de Havilland DHC-7

This aircraft, widely known as the 'Dash 7', is a short-range, STOL-capable aircraft seating up to 48 passengers and powered by four Pratt and Whitney turboprop engines. It was designed specifically for use in Canada's wilderness areas and to face the extremes of the weather it would find there. Intended to compete with the Convair 580 and HS 748, de Havilland made the decision to add oversized props, one advantage being the reduction in noise this would bring, but more impor tantly it enabled the aircraft to take on the role of a regional airliner.

The prototype made its first flight on 27 March 1975 with Rocky Mountain Airways taking delivery of the first aircraft on 3 February, 1978. The most widely produced version was the -100 regional airliner, which also came in a combi version with an additional cargo door.

Being such a specific design, particularly the STOL capabilities, and with the number of STOL ports being far fewer than had been envisaged, unfortunately meant that it wasn't a bestseller, reaching just 113 in total serving with military units, survey organisations and airlines including Tyrolean, Wardair, Maersk, Brymon, Air Niugini and Ransome Airlines. There are still thought to be a handful in service today.

FIRST FACTS	
First Flight	27/03/75
Certification	05/77
First Delivery	03/02/78
Entered service	02/78 Rocky Mountain Airways

STATS	
Length	24.58m (80ft 8in)
Height	7.98m (26ft 2in)
Wingspan	28.35m (93ft)
Typical/Max seats	50/54
Number built	113

British Aerospace Jetstream 31/41

FIRST FACTS	J31	J41
Launched	05/12/78	24/05/89
First Flight	28/03/80	25/09/91
Certification	N/A	23/11/92
First Delivery	12/82	01/92
Entered service	N/A	N/A
	Contactair	Loganair / Manx

Derived from the Handley Page Jetstream, the Jetstream 31's development began in December 1978, and it was in fact a converted Handley Page airframe that made the first flight of the J31 on 28 March, 1980. The aircraft was marketed as both a corporate transport and regional airliner, and it was the latter where it made its mark, selling particularly well in the US and fitting nicely into the niche required by the then major operators' regional affiliates. The aircraft received an upgrade with more powerful engines, the increased weights providing a better payload range performance, as well as an improved interior. This aircraft, by now named the J32, took to the air on 13 April, 1988. Shortly after, it was announced that a stretched version, the J41, was to be produced, but, probably a bit late for the market, the J41 was not as popular as its predecessor, selling less than a third of the J31/32. Making its first flight on 25 September, 1991, the J41 had been stretched by 4.88m (16ft) and been brought up to date with many systems being modernised. The launch customers of Loganair and Manx Airlines took delivery in November 1992.

STATS	J31	J41
Length	14.37m (47ft 1in)	19.25m (63ft 2in)
Height	5.38m (17ft 8in)	5.74m (18ft 10in)
Wingspan	15.85m (52ft)	18.29m (60ft)
Typical/Max seats	10/19	27/29
Number built	386	106

Dornier 228

FIRST FACTS	-100	-200
First Flight	28/03/81	09/05/81
Certification	18/12/81	N/A
Entered service	Norving	

The Dornier 228 resulted from a German government-funded research programme into new wing technology. Initially tested on a Do28 Skyservent, further work resulted in the development of the 228-100 and -200. The -100 was the first to take to the skies on 28 March, 1981, with the -200 taking its first flight on 9 May the same year. German certification came on 18 December, 1981, with Norwegian Regional airline Norving putting the first (a-100) into service in July 1982. This twin-engined general purpose aircraft is equally at home at major airports, carrying out its regional commuter role or, being STOL capable, on rough strips in hot climates. Although no airlines bought the aircraft in large numbers, its versatility, a factor Dornier marketed from the beginning, led to a total of 370 being produced, 125 of which were in India after a licence to build the aircraft was signed between Dornier and Hindustan Aeronautics Ltd in 1983. Operators varied from civilian operators as diverse as Suckling Airways in the UK to the National Cartographic Centre of Iran, to law enforcement like the Netherlands Coastguard as well as various military operators.

In 2002 Fairchild Dornier went into insolvency and RUAG Aviation division acquired the Do 228-212 type certificate, subsequently launching a next generation 228 with over 350 changes to the design.

STATS	-100	-200
Length	15.04m (49ft 4in)	16.56m (54ft 4in)
Height	4.86m (15ft 11in)	4.86m (15ft 11in)
Wingspan	16.97m (55ft 8in)	16.97m (55ft 8in)
Typical/Max seats	15/15	19/19
Number built	370 across both variants	

Ilyushin IL114

The story of this Russian (and lately Uzbekistan) built airliner is a rather protracted tale. In 1986 work began on designing a replacement for the vast number of ageing AN24s that Aeroflot were operating on domestic short-haul services.

It is a low-wing, 60-passenger aircraft powered by two turboprop engines with looks not dissimilar to the BAe ATP, and its maiden flight took place on 29 March 29, 1990. However, the programme encountered a number of problems, some technical and others due to the break-up of the Soviet Union, not least the production facility being in what would later become Uzbekistan. It was a further eight months before the second aircraft took flight, but more difficulties ensued with the crash of this aircraft leading to the withdrawal of government funding. Despite this, the project moved slowly forward, with certification being received on 26 April, 1997. Just 20 aircraft have been produced, going to Vyborg Airlines (now ceased operations) and Uzbekistan Airways, who operate the aircraft on an ad hoc basis. As is often the case with aircraft designed in the ex-Soviet bloc, there

have been a number of variants designed, from Cargo to Maritime patrol and AWACS to Arctic versions fitted with skis.

Over the years there has been noise about restoring production at various sites in Russia; however, even with a reported order for 50 of the newest version, the -300, nothing concrete has yet emerged.

FIRST FACTS	
Launched	06/86
First Flight	29/03/90
Certification	26/04/97
Entered Service	Vyborg / Uzbekistan Airways

STATS	
Length	26.88m (88ft 2in)
Height	9.32m (30ft 7in)
Wingspan	30.00m (98ft 5in)
Typical/Max seats	60/64
Number built	20

APRIL

Airbus A310

FIRST FACTS	-200	-300
First Flight	03/04/82	08/07/85
Certification	11/03/83	N/A
First Delivery	29/03/83	N/A
Entered service	12/04/83 Lufthansa	12/85 Swissair

Based on the A300, the A310 is a medium to long-range airliner, shorter than its predecessor and with a new wing along with a number of flight deck upgrades. The design goes back to the initial design studies of the A300, during which airlines had expressed an interest in a smaller version. This version ended up as the A310 and was launched on 7 July, 1978, making its first flight nearly four years later on 3 April, 1982. The cockpit was designed so that a common type rating could be achieved. By the time of this first flight, orders and options had reached over 180.

In 1985 the second version, the A310-300, made its first flight. The -300 had a greater range, made possible by additional centre and horizontal stabiliser fuel tanks, and following its first flight on 8 July it was used extensively on transatlantic routes.

The A310 has also been used by the military in both a transport and aerial refuelling capacity. The A310 became the first Airbus aircraft delivered to an Eastern Bloc airline when Interflug bought one in 1988. Another has been used as a 'vomit comet' to provide short bursts of weightlessness by Air Zero G.

STATS	-200	-300
Length	46.66m (153ft 1in)	46.66m (153ft 1in)
Height	15.80m (51ft 10in)	15.80m (51ft 10in)
Wingspan	43.9m (144ft)	43.9m (144ft)
Typical/Max seats	220/280	220/280
Number built	255 across both variants	

Boeing 737 Originals

FIRST FACTS	-100	-200
Launched	09/11/64	N/A
Rolled out	09/66	N/A
First Flight	09/04/67	08/08/67
Certification	15/12/67	21/12/67
First Delivery	28/12/67	N/A
Entered service	10/02/68 Lufthansa	28/04/68 United

The remarkable destiny of the 737 was not apparent from the beginning as sales were slow, in part due to it coming to the market somewhat late. Design work on this short/medium-haul aircraft began on 11 May, 1964 and the very first flight of the prototype of what would become the best-selling jetliner of all time took place on 9 April, 1967.

Boeing were initially looking to produce a shorter and lower cost airliner to supplement their 727 on short and thin routes. At first, the look of the aircraft was similar to the 727 but with two engines and five abreast seating. In a move to lighten the structure, the engines were placed under the wing, which had the added advantage of enabling a wider fuselage and therefore changing the layout to six abreast seating. Lufthansa became the first ever non-US airline to launch a Boeing aircraft with an order for 12, but this only came after assurances that the project would not be cancelled and that the aircraft would be able to have 100 seats. United placed an order for 40 aircraft in April of the same year, but its requirement was for a larger version, thereby leading to a stretched version which

was designated the 737-200. This aircraft flew for the first time on 8 August, 1967. Assembly of the aircraft was actually done adjacent to Boeing field as there was simply no space at Renton. On 15 December, 1967 the -100 received its certification and the first delivery was made to Lufthansa on 10 February, 1968. The -200 had also received its certification just seven days before the delivery to Lufthansa, enabling United to put it into service on 28 April, 1968. The -200 version quickly became the preferred option and only 30 of the -100 were ever produced.

By the time the 1970s arrived, things were looking a little bleak as sales had all but dried up and Boeing were considering selling the programme. However, savings made on other projects and sales to the USAF and a number of African airlines kept the production lines open and with the advent of the US Airline Deregulation act in 1978 creating a greater need for aircraft the size of the 737, the situation eventually improved. Boeing had also started offering a number of variants in a bid to boost sales: a convertible with a freight door just behind the cockpit and a gravel kit was also offered to enable the aircraft to operate from unpaved runways in remote areas, where the ability to provide service from an aircraft the size of a 737 could potentially change things massively for the local population. There was also a QC, or Quick Change, version which used palletised seating, enabling, as the name suggests, a quick change from passenger to freight use or vice versa.

Additionally, on 15 April, 1971, with a considerable number of improvements as well as the incorporation of ongoing modifications, the 737-200ADV (Advanced) took to the skies.

In the late 80s and with the 737-300, the first of the 'classic' series of 737s, already in service the decision was made to close the -200 series production line, a line that had produced 30 of the -100 version and 1,114 of the -200, with the last aircraft delivered to Xiamen Airlines in August, 1988.

STATS	-100	-200
Length	28.65m (94ft)	30.53m (100ft 2in)
Height	11.28m (37ft)	11.28m (37ft)
Wingspan	28.35m (93ft)	28.35m (93ft)
Typical seats	100/100	115/130
Number built	30	1114

LET 410

The 410 is a rugged, uncompromising twin-engine, short-range aircraft designed to meet the requirements set down by Aeroflot as an AN2 replacement. It was intended to be of all Czech manufacture, but the first few aircraft to come off the production line, including the prototype, had Pratt and Whitney engines as the Czech designed units were not ready in time. The first flight for this unpressurised 17-19 seater was on 16 April, 1969, and following testing and certification the first deliveries were made to Czech domestic airline Slov Air in the latter part of 1971. Once the Motorlet engine was ready, the standard aircraft became the L 410M, with deliveries from 1976. Aeroflot had criticised certain aspects of the design, and, given the importance of this airline to the project, LET upgraded the aircraft to have a larger wing and vertical tailplane, as well as modified spoilers and flaps and a slightly longer fuselage, making its first flight in November 1977 as the L 410UVP. Further modifications led to the L 410 UVP E taking to the skies in December 1984. By far the biggest customer was Aeroflot, who bought around three quarters of the total built. Given the solid manufacture of the aircraft and its versatility, there are a considerable number in use today, some in their original role while others have been modified as skydiving platforms.

FIRST FACTS

First Flight	16/04/69
First Delivery	1971
Entered Service	Slov Air

STATS

Length	14.42m (47ft 3in)
Height	5.97m (19ft 6in)
Wingspan	19.98m (65ft 6in)
Typical/Max seats	17/19
Number built	1,200

de Havilland Dragon Rapide

The DH.89 Dragon Rapide was the last wooden biplane produced by the de Havilland company. A mainstay for the lighter end of short haul commercial operations throughout the 1930s, it was in some ways a scaled down version of de Havilland's four-engined DH.86. It made its first flight on 17 April, 1934 with its first operator, Hillman Airways, putting it into service soon after. As with many aircraft of the period, the Second World War added considerably to the production run, with 469 of the military version, the Dominie, being produced and the vast majority of civilian versions also being pressed into service. After the end of the war many were civilianised and the aircraft once again became a regular sight at airports and flying clubs throughout the world.

FIRST FACTS

First Flight	17/04/34
First Delivery	1934
Entered service	1934 Hillman Airways

STATS

Length	10.51m (34ft 6in)
Height	3.12m (10ft 3in)
Wingspan	14.63m (48ft)
Typical seats	8
Number built	727

Lockheed L100

FIRST FACTS	L100	L100-20	L100-30	LM100J
First Flight	20/04/64	1968	08/70	25/05/17
Certification	16/02/65	04/10/68	N/A	N/A
First Delivery	30/09/65	1968	12/70	N/A
Entered service	Continental Air Svcs	Southern Air	Saturn Airways	

The L100 is Lockheed's civilian version of the ubiquitous C130 Hercules used by military forces all over the world. It made its first flight on 20 April, 1964; however, with the flight lasting 25 hours and one minute, thereby making it the longest first flight in history, it did not land until the 21st. It achieved certification on 16 February, 1965, with deliveries being made to first customer Continental Air Services on 30 September the same year. Initial sales were a little slow so Lockheed developed two stretches, the initial aircraft not having the capacity to make operations financially viable.

The L100-20 was 2.52m (8ft 4in) longer, with the -30 a further 2.03m (6ft 8in) again, the latter flying for the first time in August 1970. This stretching was a result of what is known as 'cubing out' where volumetric capacity is reached before weight limits.

It became popular with quite a number of operators, selling 114 until production was stopped in 1992. A new design based on the current C130J, which had been placed on hold in 2000, was re-launched in 2015 and the aircraft took to the skies on 25 May, 2017.

STATS	L100	L100-20	L100-30	LM100J
Length	29.79m (97ft 9in)	32.33m (106ft 1in)	34.37m (112ft 9in)	34.36m (112ft 9in
Height	11.66m (36ft 3in)	11.66m (36ft 3in)	11.66m (36ft 3in)	11.84m (38ft 10in)
Wingspan	40.41m (132ft 7in)	40.41m (132ft 7in)	40.41m (132ft 7in)	40.41m (132ft 7in)
No. built	22	27	66	N/A

Airbus A380

FIRST FACTS	
Launched	19/12/00
Rolled out	18/01/05
First Flight	27/04/05
Certification	12/12/06
First Delivery	15/10/07
Entered service	28/10/07
	Singapore Airlines

The A380 is probably one of the best-known commercial aircraft flying today, still turning heads as it floats gracefully into the world's airports. Work on the A380 can be traced back as far as 1994 when the project was still called the A3XX. It wasn't until December 1999 that the Airbus board authorised the go ahead for the programme, with the commercial launch happening in June 2000 and the A380 designation being confirmed on 12 December, 2000. Further design and manufacturing of the first sections was completed over the following years and they were all transported to

the Final Assembly Line (FAL) in Toulouse by April 2004. The aircraft was rolled out on 18 January, 2005, with the historic first flight completed just three months later on 27 April.

Not everything was 'plane' sailing though. In the middle of 2006, when 15 aircraft had already been assembled, Airbus realised that it had problems with the installation of wiring harnesses resulting from a combination of late changes in customer cabin specifications and modifications deemed necessary from information acquired during the test programme, the remedy to which affected delivery schedules for approximately two years. Furthermore, the initial delivery to launch customer Singapore Airlines was also delayed until October 2007. The need to fix the various issues had an unfortunate side effect. By prioritising work on the passenger version, this led to further delays on the freighter version and the subsequent cancellation of orders from FedEx and UPS, which effectively stopped the freight programme in its tracks.

Once in the air and in passenger service, it was loved by those who flew it, in all cabins. The cabin felt spacious and internal noise was noticeably low. Airlines had made an effort to set new standards by making use of the large available space.

Designed to transport 525 passengers on distances up to 14,816km (9,206 miles), this double-decker airliner's early marketing suggested the possible addition of casinos, gyms or even beauty parlours. Unfortunately, the simple economics of operating the aircraft took precedence and such areas were never produced, seats are what pay the bills after all. What the airlines that operate the aircraft have done is to hone the premier product with ever-better seats and surroundings and then market these as a benefit of flying their A380. A bar or communal seating area is something that many operators have in their A380s, but some have gone that extra bit further. Emirates, the world's largest operator of the type, introduced the first-ever on-board shower for use by first-class guests. Etihad have taken this a stage further with what they term 'The Residence'. They have created what is in effect a completely separate room complete with butler! Not only does it have a separate first-class bathroom and shower, this 'Residence' features a separate living room, bathroom and double bedroom, using just 125 square feet. In addition, there are also the first apartments which have a separate armchair and bed plus wardrobe and drinks/vanity cabinets.

Everything about this aircraft is big, from its design and production costs to the buildings in which it is constructed. The basis of construction does not vary from the Airbus norm in that it is constructed in various sections at Airbus sites across Europe and then transported to Toulouse for final assembly.

However, when it came to the A380, Airbus had to think differently about how it would get the major components to the Toulouse FAL. Although certain components of the forward fuselage and vertical tailplane of the A380 could be transported to Blagnac by Beluga, the dimensions of the other components mean that they simply would not fit and Airbus therefore had to develop a multimodal transport solution involving ships, barges and trucks.

Therefore, the wings from Broughton in North Wales, the fuselage sections from Hamburg in Germany and Saint Nazaire in France and the

horizontal tail plane from Cadiz in Spain are all transported by sea and inland waterways to Langon in France. From there the six components are carefully loaded onto specially designed and constructed trailers which are then hauled by trucks over two nights over the 240km Itinéraries à Grand Gabaret (ITGG), loosely translated as 'oversized convoy route', to Toulouse – a spectacular sight in itself with many people coming out in the small hours to witness the huge components being transported through small French villages, often with what looks like millimetres between the convoy and buildings.

Once the aircraft has been assembled it is flown to the Airbus site at Finkenwerder in Hamburg to fit the cabin and for painting. This is also the first flight of this airframe and is therefore a test flight primarily, albeit with Finkenwerder as its destination.

There are 15 operators of the aircraft, with Emirates being by far the biggest. As at May 2018, 331 aircraft had been ordered with 162 of these heading to Emirates. The launch customer was Singapore Airlines, whose first service was introduced on 25 October, 2007. The newest operator is All Nippon Airways (ANA). However, there are a number of orders that are likely to be at risk, with airlines having changed their minds or suffering from financial difficulties. Orders have slumped somewhat in recent years from a peak of 42 in 2013, although Emirates firmed up an order (and options) for an additional 36 aircraft in 2018. Operating airlines use the aircraft on predominantly long-haul operations, the longest of which is an Emirates service from Dubai to Auckland. However, it has also been used by Air France on its Paris-London Heathrow route (344km/214 miles) and more recently an Emirates rotation from Dubai to Doha (379km/236 miles).

Unfortunately for Airbus, QANTAS and much more significantly, Emirates, cancelled or reduced orders early in 2019 which left the company with no option but to make the "painful" decision to cancel the programme with the last expected delivery at the end of 2021. The future was already looking a little uncertain with early models retired by Singapore Airlines in danger of being broken up rather than finding a second home. So far just one second-hand aircraft has been placed, with Hi Fly of Portugal. This is partly due to these aircraft not having the various weight savings and other modifications made over the course of its production. The cost to refurbish and reconfigure is potentially prohibitive.

STATS	
Length	72.80m (238ft 10in)
Height	24.10m (79ft 1in)
Wingspan	79.80m (261ft 10in)
Typical/Max seats	544/868
Number ordered	250 (02/19)

Boeing 747-400

This month seems heavily linked with first flights from large commercial airliners, as the 747-400 also made its maiden flight this month in 1988. This version became the best-selling of all of the 747 line and with sales for the newest version being slow to say the least, it is likely to remain so.

There were a number of changes and improvements over the previous -300 version, the most significant of which was more efficient engines, linked with increased fuel capacity, and aerodynamic tweaks that provided the aircraft with a greater range. Up front there is now a two-crew digital flight deck and behind that an upgraded cabin design. Most noticeable externally is the addition of winglets on an increased wingspan. Certification was achieved on 9 January, 1989 with Northwest Airlines taking the first aircraft just a few weeks later on the 26th.

Various versions have been produced including full and combo freighters, as well as another similar to the -300SR, although this time named the -400D (for domestic), again optimised for use in the Japanese short-haul market. This aircraft did not have any winglets.

The Queen of the Skies, as it has become known, is slowly becoming a rarer sight now as more fuel efficient long-range twins are now the norm. It is, though, still in service with many of the world's flag carriers, including BA, Lufthansa QANTAS and Korean Air; however, most have their retirement planned. The freighter versions are likely to stay in operation for many more years.

FIRST FACTS

Launched	10/85
Rolled out	01/88
First Flight	29/04/88
Certification	10/01/89
First Delivery	26/01/89 Northwest
Entered service	09/02/89 Northwest

STATS

Length	70.66m (231ft 10in)
Height	19.41m (63ft 8in)
Wingspan	64.44m (211ft 5in)
Typical/Max seats	420/568
Number built	694

MAY

COMAC C919

WEIMENG

Launched in May 2008, the C919 was the first large commercial aircraft to be developed under the auspices of COMAC. It was designed to compete in a market dominated by the Boeing 737MAX and Airbus A320neo, and by February 2018 its order book had reached 815, mainly from Chinese operators. Although ostensibly a Chinese product, there is a great reliance on foreign suppliers for parts including engines and avionics, but with the majority of the airframe is Chinese built and the aircraft is to be assembled in Shanghai.

The first flight was initially planned for 2014; however, a number of technical and supply issues pushed this back. The aircraft was eventually rolled out on 2 November, 2015 but it was still some considerable time before the aircraft first flew on 5 May, 2017. There has been limited flight testing since and entry into service is stated to be 2021, which in itself is a considerable amount of time. It will be interesting to see if first customer China Eastern Airlines will receive their aircraft on time.

FIRST FACTS	
Launched	05/08
Rolled out	02/11/15
First Flight	05/05/17

STATS	
Length	38.90m (127ft 7in)
Height	11.95m (39ft 2in)
Wingspan	35.78m (117ft 5in)
Typical/Max seats	156/168
Number Built	2 (prototypes)

Fokker F28

FIRST FACTS	1000	2000	3000	4000
Announced	04/62	N/A	N/A	N/A
Rolled out	N/A	N/A	N/A	20/10/76
First Flight	09/05/67	28/04/71	N/A	N/A
Certification	24/02/69	N/A	N/A	N/A
First Delivery	02/69 LTU	10/72 Nigeria A/W	07/77 Garuda	12/76 Linjeflyg
Entered service	28/03/69 Braathens			

The F28 Fellowship was designed to complement the turboprop F27 and was announced by Fokker in 1962. It was to be in collaboration with MBB, Fokker-VFW and Shorts. It was initially expected to be a 50-seater and looked like both the BAC 1-11 and Douglas DC9 with a T-tail and rear fuselage-mounted engines. It had, by the time of the launch in 1965, increased to upwards of 65 seats. Components were transported to Amsterdam's Schipol airport for final assembly and the prototype first took to Dutch skies on 9 May, 1967. Launch customer LTU took delivery of the first aircraft, which by then had been given the designation of F28-1000, in February 1969. It was, however, Braathens who first put the aircraft into service on 28 March, 1969. Fokker went on to produce a Mk2000, which was stretched to accommodate up to 79 passengers, and this aircraft's maiden flight was on 28 April, 1971. The most successful of the variants were the Mk3000 and 4000, the latter being put into service by Linjeflyg on 20 October, 1976. Seating up to 85, it was powered by quieter Spey engines, had a new cockpit and larger wingspan. A Mk6000 was produced and flew for the first time on 27 September, 1973 but was never really successful. Production ended in 1987, by which time 241 of all marques had been constructed.

STATS	1000	2000	3000	4000
Length	27.40m (89ft 11in)	29.61m (97ft 2in)	27.40m (89ft 11in)	29.61m (97ft 2in)
Height	8.47m (27ft 9in)	8.47m (27ft 9in)	8.47m (27ft 9in)	8.47m (27ft 9in)
Wingspan	23.58m (77ft 4in)	23.58m (77ft 4in)	25.07m (82ft 3in)	25.07m (82ft 3in)
Typical/Max seats	55/65	79/79	55/65	85/85
Total No built	241 across all variants			

Bombardier CRJ100/200

FIRST FACTS	-100	-200
Launched	31/03/89	N/A
Rolled out	06/05/91	N/A
First Flight	10/05/91	1995
Certification	31/07/92	N/A
First Delivery	29/10/92 Lufthansa CityLine	15/01/96 Tyrolean Airways
Entered Service	01/11/92 Lufthansa CityLine	N/A Tyrolean Airways

Based on the Challenger business jet the Canadair (and latterly Bombardier), CRJ was designed for the growing market for regional jets. The programme got its go ahead on 31 March,1989 with preparatory work stretching back as far as 1981 when the company first looked at the possibilities of producing a jet airliner with the economics of a turboprop. The first of the eventual three development aircraft made the first flight on 10 May, 1991 and it achieved US certification on 24 July, 1991. Lufthansa's Cityline division were the launch customers, taking delivery of the first of the 50-seat aircraft on 29 October, 1992.

Other versions with higher weights and fuel capacity (100ER and 100LR) were joined in 1995 by the -200, which had more efficient engines. Both versions received orders both in Europe and perhaps most importantly in the USA, with the likes of ASA, Express Jet, Sky West Airlines and Air Wisconsin, often to operate on behalf of their major airline affiliates. Interestingly, this airliner from a biz jet often found itself being purchased as a corporate shuttle. Once the final -200 was delivered in 2006, a total of 1,021 had been built, including 86 of the 44-seat -440 only purchased by Northwest Airlines.

STATS	-100	-200
Length	26.77m (87ft 10in)	26.77m (87ft 10in)
Height	6.22m (20ft 5in)	6.22m (20ft 5in)
Wingspan	21.21m (69ft 7in)	21.21m (69ft 7in)
Typical/Max seats	50/52	50/52
Number Built	226	709

de Havilland DH.114 Heron

Based on the smaller light feeder airliner DH.104 Dove, the four-engined stretched Heron could transport up to 17 passengers over distances of up to 1,126km (700miles), although standard configuration was for 14 passengers. The toilet needed to be removed and baggage space reduced to make room for the extra three. There were two basic models offered. The Srs 1 had a fixed tricycle for short hops as speed was naturally reduced, and this was the first to fly on 10 May, 1950, with first deliveries being made in April 1952 to New Zealand National Airways and to Braathens in May. Other operators included Garuda and BEA.

The Srs 1 was, however, somewhat underpowered and de Havilland upgraded the design to include more powerful engines and a retractable undercarriage. The Srs 2, as it was designated, first flew on 14 December, 1952, with the first three deliveries all being made with a VIP/corporate layout, including one to the Saudi Royal family. In fact, it gained further Royal approval when the British Queen's Flight took one aircraft. Braathens was the first airline to take delivery, their aircraft arriving in January 1955. Other users included Jersey Airlines, Cambrian Airways in the UK, Toa Airways in Japan and Primair of Puerto Rico.

Even when the last of the 150 aircraft rolled off the de Havilland Chester plant in 1963, there was still a long career ahead of the type as several companies performed conversions which saw them flying as late as 2012.

FIRST FACTS

First Flight	10/05/50
Certification	11/50
First delivery	04/52
	New Zealand National Airways

STATS

Length	14.78m (48ft 6in)
Height	4.75m (15ft 7in)
Wingspan	21.79m (71ft 6in)
Typical/Max seats	14/17
Number Built	150

Douglas DC2

The DC2 benefitted from a TWA specification for a three-engined, all-metal monoplane coupled with a difficulty in obtaining the Boeing 247 due to United Airlines monopoly of the type. Despite it having only two engines, the DC1 flew on 1 July, 1933, and after a series of flights they had made enough of a case to convince TWA to order 20. By now the designation was DC2, which meant that there was only ever one DC1 produced.

The slightly longer DC2 could seat 14 passengers and first flew on 11 May, 1934, with the first aircraft being delivered just one week later. The aircraft was fast becoming popular and orders came in from many of the then major US airlines as well as Swissair and KLM in Europe. In fact, Fokker assembled 39 DC2s under licence in the early 1930s, with the total number produced nearing 200.

Such was the leap in technology that a DC2 that KLM entered into the October 1934 MacRobertson Air race between London and Melbourne, Australia, came second, but only to a purpose-built race aircraft.

FIRST FACTS	
First Flight	11/05/34
First delivery	18/05/34
	TWA

STATS	
Length	18.89m (62ft)
Height	4.97m (16ft 4in)
Wingspan	25.91m (85ft)
Typical/Max seats	14/14
Number Built	198

Sukhoi Superjet 100

The roots of this Russian-built regional airliner go back to 2001 when the Russian Aviation and Space agency Rosaviakosmos and Boeing signed a co-operation agreement which included the development of a family of regional jets. In October 2004 the programme was given the green light, by which time Boeing had signed a further agreement with the winning bidder, Sukhoi. By the time of the first order at the 2005 Moscow Airshow, the programme had become a much more international affair, with major subcontractors involved from all around the globe.

Originally planned as a family, the sizes of the SSJ were down to just two, one seating 75 and the other 95, with the latter initially becoming the baseline version (later on this was the 100-75 version). Now known as the Superjet 100, the aircraft was gaining orders, and not just from the Russian Federation. A total of 73 were on order by the time of the first flight on 19 May, 2008. Armavia was to be the launch customer and they received the first production aircraft on 19 April, 2011 after it had made its maiden flight five months earlier, with type certification being received in February 2011. Aeroflot made the largest order of 30 aircraft.

FIRST FACTS	-95
Launched	12/03/03
Rolled out	26/09/07
First Flight	19/05/08
Certification	28/01/11
First Delivery	19/04/11
	Armavia
Entered Service	21/04/11
	Armavia

Unfortunately, the introduction of the aircraft was not a smooth one, with a number of mechanical incidents creating a reported despatch reliability of just 95.4 per cent for Aeroflot in 2012. Even worse that year was the crash of a demonstration aircraft in Indonesia with the loss of 37 passengers and eight crew. There was more bad news in July 2013 when a wheels-up landing was made at Keflavik during Cat IIIA landing trials.

Despite these setbacks, the aircraft continued to gain orders and certification in other countries, enabling Interjet of Mexico to take delivery of their first aircraft in May 2013, although the continuing difficulty with spare parts also led to aircraft unservicability. Other operators include Yamal Airlines, UT Air, Gazpromavia and City Jet, as well as a number of VIP configured private jets.

STATS	-95
Length	29.94m (98ft 3in)
Height	10.28m (33ft 9in)
Wingspan	27.80m (91ft 2in)
Typical/Max seats	87/108
Number Delivered	147 (April 2019)
Number Ordered	418

de Havilland DHC-6 Twin Otter

FIRST FACTS	
Launched	1964
First Flight	20/05/65

A replacement for the DHC-3 Otter, the DHC-6 Twin Otter retained the STOL capabilities of its predecessor and, despite being originally designed for the wild areas of the Canadian north, it went on to become one of the most successful post-war light transports, operated in over 80 countries.

Development began in 1964 and built on the success of the single-engined Otter by stretching the fuselage and using the same basic wing, albeit larger and with a tricycle undercarriage. The single-piston engine was replaced by two more reliable turboprops, hence the name Twin Otter.

The aircraft first flew on 20 May, 1965, with deliveries being made a mere three months later. Early operators like Pilgrim Airlines and Air Wisconsin soon saw what an impact the aircraft was to have on the regional airline industry, particularly in the US. However, it was not only used in North America for regional ops or bush flying.

Around the globe, 80 operators purchased the aircraft for a variety of uses. Although the majority of sales (500) were to third level or regional airlines, hundreds were used for different uses from medevac and SAR to survey and relief agencies to military operators.

Such is the versatility of the aircraft that it can be delivered with floats or skis instead of the standard undercarriage. The aircraft can be operated from bushstrips to STOL ports and snow strips to water, as well as the odd Scottish beach!

Initial production versions were designated series 100. The series 200 was next, which had an increased cargo capacity in a lengthened nose.

However, the vast majority of sales came from the series 300 model, which had more powerful PT6A-27 engines and an increased maximum weight, as well as room for 20 passengers, one more than the previous versions. This version first took to the skies in May 1969, and by the time production ended in 1988 614 of this latter version (and country specific subvariants) had been sold out of a total of 844.

This was not the end of the Twin Otter story, however. Viking Air purchased the tooling for the aircraft and in February 2006 also purchased the type certificates, leading to an announcement at that year's Farnborough Airshow of the intention to produce a new (series 400) version of the popular twin.

Production restarted at a new plant in Calgary and, following a first flight on 1 October, 2008, Zimex Aviation of Switzerland received the first of the 'new' aircraft in July 2010. The aircraft has been brought up to date with new avionics and a modernised electrical and lighting system, as well as the use of composites.

STATS	
Length	15.77m (51ft 9in)
Height	5.90m (19ft 4in)
Wingspan	19.80m (65ft)
Typical/Max seats	19/20
Number Built	844 (Original production run)
Number Built	125 (New production)

Embraer E2 Series

FIRST FACTS	175E2	190E2	195E2
Rolled out	N/A	25/02/16	03/07/17
First Flight	N/A	23/05/16	29/03/17
Certification	N/A	28/02/18	28/02/18
First Delivery	N/A	04/04/18	N/A
	N/A	Wideroe	N/A
Entered service	N/A	24/04/18	N/A
	N/A	Wideroe	N/A

Embraer launched the revamp of its popular E jet range at the Paris Airshow in 2013. There are three variants, all sharing the same fuselage cross section, with lengths broadly matching the previous versions. The first to fly was the E190E2, taking off on its maiden voyage on 23 May, 2016, somewhat earlier than planned. Flight testing continued in the same fashion with better than expected performance in a number of areas. Following certification on 28 February, 2018 the first delivery was made to Wideroe on 4 April, 2018, entering service 20 days later. The next variant had by this time made its first flight, which took place on 29 March, 2017, and Azul had been announced as the launch customer. The smallest of this new trio will be the E175E2, which has yet to make its first flight.

STATS	175E2	190E2	195E2
Length	32.40m (106ft 3in)	36.24m (118ft 11in)	41.50m (136ft 2in)
Height	9.98m (32ft 7in)	10.95m (35ft 11in)	10.90m (35ft 8in)
Wingspan	31.00m (101ft 7in)	33.72m (110ft 8in)	35.10m (115ft 2in)
Total ordered (02/19)	100	47	114
Typical/Max seats	80/90	96/114	120/146

Sud Aviation SE 210 Caravelle

FIRST FACTS	PROTOTYPE	11R	10B	12
First Flight	27/05/55	21/04/67	31/08/64	12/03/71
First Delivery	N/A	N/A	N/A	N/A
		N/A	Finnair	Sterling

The Caravelle came into existence because of a requirement from the French government for an aircraft capable of carrying 55-65 passengers and 1,000kg of freight over what was termed 'medium range'. The eventual winning design by Sud Est (then Sud Aviation and later Aerospatiale) included a number of firsts. Most notable, it was the first short-medium range jet airliner, but it was also the first to have twin engines mounted at the rear and to have a rear airstair incorporated in the tail. Having been ordered in 1953, the first of two prototypes took to French skies over the historic Toulouse site on 27 May, 1955. This short timespan was helped considerably by co-operation with de havilland after the design of the Comet cockpit was licensed to the French company, meaning a huge saving in design time and the acquisition of tried and tested technology. The aircraft also had trian-

gular windows on the presumption that passengers would be predominantly looking down. This design kept the view for the passenger whilst keeping a greater strength in the design, an important point considering the recent difficulties caused by the Comet windows.

This first flight was eventful in two very different ways. Firstly, having encountered difficulties with the flaps once airborne, the flight time was cut short, and, secondly, on board was the first-ever passenger acting as an extra engineer, a man named Roger Béteille, who at the time was head of flight test for Sud Est but would in later years become one of Airbus's founding fathers.

By the time of the very first delivery to the launch customer Finnair on 18 February, 1960, Sud Est had merged with Sud Ouest to become Sud Aviation and the aircraft was named the Caravelle 1, which had a slightly longer nose section housing a weather station. This first production model made its first flight on 18 May, 1958. Users of the early versions were extensive. Air France were a major operator of the type throughout, as well as many other European majors. Further afield, Royal Air Maroc had a number of aircraft.

Like many designs, the Caravelle was modified to provide greater power from the engines and allow increased weights, as well as being stretched for more passengers. The first of these was the Caravelle III, which took to the air in December 1959. The VI-N was next to enter service with Sabena, and the final Avon powered version, the VI-R, broke into the American market with United Airlines taking 20.

This latter version, in addition to greater power, also had improvements to the windscreen and brakes, as well as the addition of thrust reversers and spoilers. These later versions found homes all around the world. In addition to United in North America, South American operators like Cruzeiro do Sul, LAN Chile, Panair do Brasil and Aerolineas Argentinas took delivery of this new jet.

The Caravelle 10B had more powerful Pratt and Whitney engines and the 11R was stretched

by 0.84m (2ft 4in) allowing for up to 19 more passengers over the original's 80. Further stretches to the 10B and 12 took passenger numbers up to 140. These 'second generation' versions earned the name Super Caravelle. Sterling Airways, LTU, Air Inter and Aero Lloyd were all users of these versions.

In the end there were nine variants, selling 280 in total (plus two prototypes), 80 more than the break-even point set by Sud Aviation. The aircraft was quite long lived as well, with the final example to make a commercial flight only retiring in 2005.

STATS	PROTOTYPE TO 10R	11R	10B	12
Length	32.00m (105ft)	32.71m (107ft 4in)	33.01m (108ft 3in)	36.23m (118ft 10in)
Height	8.71m (28ft 7in)	8.71m (28ft 7in)	9.02m (29ft 7in)	9.02m (29ft 7in)
Wingspan	34.29m (112ft 6in)	34.29m (112ft 6in)	34.29m (112ft 6in)	34.29m (112ft 6in)
Typical/Max seats	64/80	89/99	94/104	118/128
Total No built	242	6	22	12

Dassault Breguet Mercure

I FWIS GRANT

This twin-engined, single aisle airliner was conceived as a competitor to Boeing's 737; however, it proved not to be much of a challenger. Only 12 were ever built and all were operated by just one airline, Air Inter.

Initially the design was based on a 110-120-seater with rear-mounted engines; however, this evolved into a 150-seater with under wing slung engines. Officially launched in 1969, it was the first large pan-European civil aeronautical programme. Dassault was a successful manufacturer of military aircraft but this was their first venture into the commercial market, and it was seen as an opportunity to demonstrate their expertise, whilst following their philosophy of producing a product that they considered would supply an underserved market.

Rolled out on 4 April, 1971, the aircraft lifted off from the Mérignac runway for the first time on 28 May that year. Air Inter placed what turned out to be the first and only order on 30 January, 1972 with the first of these 10 production aircraft flying on 19 July, 1973 and certification following on 12 February, 1974. In an unplanned nod to the future, the very first flight was from Paris Orly to Toulouse, which of course now houses the headquarters of the pan-European aircraft manufacturer, Airbus.

Dassault tried very hard to get airlines interested in the aircraft, but a combination of an oil cri-

FIRST FACTS	
Launched	10/04/69
Rolled out	04/04/71
First Flight	28/05/71
Certification	12/02/74
First Delivery	1974 Air Inter
Entered Service	04/06/74 Air Inter

STATS	
Length	34.84m (114ft 4in)
Height	11.36m (37ft 3in)
Wingspan	30.55m (100ft 3in)
Typical/Max seats	150/162
Number Built	12

sis reducing new aircraft demand, devaluation of the US Dollar, a higher rate of inflation in Europe than in the US, competition from the established Boeing and Douglas and the aircraft perhaps not being what the airlines needed at that time meant it struggled. Although a perfectly good airliner, all of this led to what was arguably the worst commercial aviation failure of all time. The last flight of a Mercure was on 29 April, 1995.

Bombardier CRJ700/900/1000

FIRST FACTS	-700	-900	-1000
First Flight	29/05/99	21/02/01	03/09/08
First Delivery	31/01/01	30/01/03	13/12/10
Entered service	08/02/01 Brit Air	26/04/03 Mesa Air	12/10 Air Nostrum / Brit Air

With the success of the CRJ100/200 in the 50-75-seater market, Bombardier decided to take on the larger regional aircraft market and go up against Fokker 70/100 and BAE 146/RJ. Officially launched in 1977, the CRJ700 has a slightly wider fuselage than the CRJ200 it is based on and is stretched by 5.64m (18ft 6in). This new version also had a modified wing and undercarriage, more powerful engines and it carried up to 78 passengers. Brit Air put the first aircraft into service in 2001. A further stretch occurred with the addition of the CRJ900, which made its first flight on 21 February, 2001, again from Montreal Mirabel Airport. This version had some modifications but was essentially the same as the previous one, other than the stretch, which took the passenger total to 90. The launch customer was Mesa Air Group.

The longest of the family, the CRJ1000, which can seat up to 100 passengers, made its maiden flight on 3 September, 2008; however, a fault with the rudder controls caused a delay in the flight test programme, meaning that certification wasn't achieved until 10 November, 2010. Deliveries to launch customers Air Nostrum and Brit Air were made in the week of 13 December, 2010. This next generation of CRJs went on to sell to airlines all around the world, with major operators being US based including Skywest Airlines, Endeavour Air and PSA. Lufthansa and SAS in addition to launch customer Air Nostrum are major users in Europe. As at June 2018, there are 893 on order.

STATS	-700	-900	-1000
Length	32.30m (106ft 1in)	36.20m (118ft 11in)	39.10m (128ft 5in)
Height	7.60m (24ft 10in)	7.50m (24ft 7in)	7.50m (24ft 7in)
Wingspan	23.20m (76ft 3in)	24.90m (81ft 7in)	26.20m (85ft 11in)
Typical/Max seats	66/78	76/90	97/104
No. ordered (12/18)	346	478	63

Douglas DC8

FIRST FACTS	10	20	30	40
Launched	07/55	N/A	N/A	N/A
Rolled out	09/04/58	N/A	N/A	N/A
First Flight	30/05/58	29/11/58	21/02/59	03/06/59
Certification	08/59	N/A	N/A	N/A
First Delivery	06/59 United Airlines	01/60 Eastern Airlines	02/60 Pan Am	N/A
Entered service	18/09/59 Delta	N/A	N/A	N/A

The DC8 was essentially designed as a competitor to the Boeing 707, even though Douglas was not initially convinced about the future of pure jet airliners, with turboprop aircraft like the Vickers Viscount, Lockheed Electra and the Bristol Britannia all proving popular with both airlines and their passengers and the first jet airliner, the Comet, having been grounded. This, combined with the expected higher cost and ongoing technical challenges, made Douglas nervous.

That said, Boeing were pushing ahead with the 707 and the thought process was that if airlines started to buy this new jet in numbers, could the others afford not to? Therefore, in an attempt to take some of this potential market share, Douglas launched the DC8 in July 1955. Earlier designs were for a four-engined aircraft carrying just 80 passengers; however, by the time of its launch the aircraft's four engines were now carrying 177 people. The decision to go forward soon turned

STATS	10	20	30	40
Length	45.87m (150ft 6in)	45.87m (150ft 6in)	45.87m (150ft 6in)	45.87m (150ft 6in)
Height	12.90m (42ft 4in)	12.90m (42ft 4in)	12.90m (42ft 4in)	12.90m (42ft 4in)
Wingspan	43.40m (142ft 4in)	43.40m (142ft 4in)	43.40m (142ft 4in)	43.40m (142ft 4in)
Typical/Max seats	132/179	132/179	132/179	132/179
Total No built	28	34	57	32

FIRST FACTS	50	61	62	63
First Flight	20/12/60	14/03/66	29/08/66	10/04/67
Certification	05/61	09/66	N/A	N/A
First Delivery	05/61	N/A	N/A	N/A
	KLM	N/A	N/A	N/A
Entered service	N/A	02/67	05/67	07/68
	KLM	United	SAS	KLM

out to be correct when Pan Am placed an order for 25 airframes (in addition to 20 707s) in October 1955. Although not the first order, which was from National Airlines, it was the catalyst that set in motion the need for other airlines to follow suit, with orders coming from major airlines in both the USA and Europe.

Initial versions were the Srs 10 (Domestic), Srs 20 (Hot and high) and the Srs 30 intercontinental that carried substantially more fuel to enable the required distances.

The aircraft was rolled out at the Long Beach plant on 9 April, 1958 and made its maiden flight on 30 May the same year. In an attempt to catch up with Boeing, whose 707 was much further on in its development, Douglas committed 10 aircraft to the certification phase and achieved it in August 1959. In the testing phase and during a controlled dive on 21 August, 1961, the DC8 became the first commercial transport aircraft to break the sound barrier.

The aircraft entered service with both Delta and United on 18 September, 1959. Douglas had

previously refused to offer the aircraft in a variety of sizes but eventually realised that they simply could not continue with this course of action. The series 40 and 50 versions were essentially re-engined, the 40 with Rolls Royce Conway Turbofans and the 50 with the JT3D, the engine of choice for most 707 operators. So, it wasn't until the Srs 60 that there was much visible difference, with this version being over 11 metres longer. This version (Srs 61 aimed at US domestic operations) first flew on 14 March, 1966, with certification following that September, allowing deliveries to first operator United in January 1967. This version could carry up to 259 passengers, although more often was configured for between 180 and 220. Further variants followed, with cargo doors and increased weights. The Srs 62 had a longer range with shorter stretch, and the Srs63 combined the stretch of the 61 with the range of the 62. In later years, these '60' variants were re-engined with high bypass turbofans and consequently renamed as '70s'.

STATS	50	61	62	63
Length	45.87m (150ft 6in)	57.10m (187ft 4in)	47.98m (157ft 5in)	57.10m (187ft 4in)
Height	12.90m (42ft 4in)	12.93m (42ft 5in)	12.93m (42ft 5in)	12.93m (42ft 5in)
Wingspan	43.40m (142ft 4in)	43.40m (142ft 4in)	45.20m (148ft 4in)	45.20m (148ft 4in)
Typical/Max seats	132/189	210/269	132/189	210/269
Total built	143	88	67	107

JUNE

Shorts SD360

Following on from the success of the SD330, Shorts had been studying a stretched version of the 330 that was to have more powerful engines with higher weights and consequently a larger capacity. The latter was important as deregulation in the US during 1978 had relaxed the rule that stipulated commuter aircraft could not have more than 30 seats. Feeling that the 330 had a rather outdated look and that the need for a rear loading ramp was not a requirement for this new design, Shorts introduced a more modern look with a single tail unit on a redesigned, more 'normal', tapered rear fuselage that also had the advantage of reduced drag. The aircraft could still operate from runways as short as 1,400m (4,500ft) meaning many airports were now accessible.

The product launch was in January 1981 and the first flight was made just five months later on 1 June, 1981, with certification coming on 2 September, 1982. It was in the USA that the first deliveries were again made, with Suburban Airlines taking delivery in November 1982. There were two subsequent versions of the 360. The 200 series had more powerful engines and flew for the first time in October 1985 before deliveries began with Thai International, and the final version, the 300 series, used engines of a similar power, now driving six-bladed props, but they had been

FIRST FACTS	
Launched	01/81
First Flight	01/06/81
First Delivery	11/82
	Suburban Airlines

de-rated for use in hot and high conditions. In addition, there were modifications to the wing struts and cabin interior, as well as an optional autopilot system. The first flight for this version was in February 1987, with Philippine Airlines taking the first aircraft in April 1987. Although very popular in the UK and USA, other operators of the aircraft came from all parts of the globe and included CAAC of China, LAPA from Argentina, Rheinland Air Service from Germany and Hazelton and Sunstate Airlines (QANTASLink) from Australia. Production of the aircraft finished in 1991 after 165 deliveries.

STATS	
Length	21.58m (70ft 10in)
Height	7.27m (23ft 10in)
Wingspan	22.80m (74ft 10in)
Typical/Max seats	36/36
Number built	165

Boeing 777

FIRST FACTS	200	200ER	300	300ER
Launched	29/10/90	29/10/90	26/06/95	29/02/00
First order	15/10/90	14/06/91	14/06/95	31/03/00
Rolled out	09/04/94	21/08/96	08/09/97	14/11/02
First Flight	12/06/94	07/10/96	16/10/97	24/02/03
Certification	19/04/95	17/01/97	04/05/98	16/03/04
First Delivery	15/05/95 United	06/02/97 BA	22/05/98 Cathay Pacific	29/04/04 Air France
Entered service	07/07/95 United	09/02/97 BA	27/05/98 Cathay Pacific	N/A N/A

The triple seven was originally known as the 767-X as it was to be a stretched version of the popular twin jet. However, airline feedback was such that an all-new design with a wider fuselage was developed with a host of new technologies, including Boeing's first venture into fly by wire, as well as the use of composite materials and an advanced glass cockpit. The programme was officially launched following an order from United in October 1990. Boeing saw it as a replacement for the DC10 and Tristar, as well as some early model 747s as it was expected to have operating

cost savings of up to 35 per cent over the 747. Although later dropped, it also initially had the option of folding wing tips to reduce gate width requirements, something that Boeing have now re-introduced in the latest model – the 777X. It was initially offered in two variants, the standard -200 and an increased weight, longer-range version subsequently called the -200ER.

The aircraft rolled out of the factory on 9 April, 1994 and performed its maiden flight less than two months later on 12 June. This first flight was with Pratt and Whitney engines and subsequent first flights were made with both GE and RR engines. Certification of the original PW powered aircraft was achieved just over a year from roll out on 19 April, 1995; furthermore, it also achieved 180 minutes ETOPS just a month later. Launch customer United received their first aircraft on 15 May, 1995, putting it into service on 7 June on the Washington to London route. Other early users of the aircraft were British Airways, All Nippon, China Southern Airlines and Thai Airways international. The aircraft could carry up to 440 passengers in a high-density layout, although a three-class configuration would more likely hold 305.

The first major evolution of the airframe came in 1995 when the Boeing board launched the -300 in late June after being revealed at the Paris Airshow earlier in the month. This initial stretch sacrificed some range for extra capacity, now matching that of early 747-100/200s. It took to the skies on 16 October, 1997, with the first delivery going to Cathay Pacific on 22 May, 1998.

This lost range was recouped with the introduction of the -300ER, which made its first flight

on 24 February, 2003 and Air France (via ILFC) took the first delivery on 29 April the following year. This version went on to outsell all the other versions combined.

In total, 1,559 777-200/300 have been delivered and a further 101 are currently on order. The aircraft has also been successful as an all-out freighter, with nearly 200 orders being placed. These figures do not include the newest addition to the family, the 777X, which is currently in production and has 326 on order, taking the complete 777 order total to a very respectable 1,986.

STATS	200	200ER	300	300ER
Length	63.73m (209ft 1in)	63.73m (209ft 1in)	73.86m (242ft 4in)	73.86m (242ft 4in)
Height	18.75m (61ft 6in)	18.75m (61ft 6in)	18.49m (60ft 8in)	18.49m (60ft 8in)
Wingspan	60.93m (199ft 11in)	60.93m (199ft 11in)	64.80m (212ft 7in)	64.80m (212ft 7in)
Typical/Max seats	305/440	305/440	400/550	400/550
Total No ordered	88	422 (+59LR +194F)	60	837

Britten Norman BN2A Islander

Initially designed to replace the de Havilland Dragon Rapide, it had STOL characteristics and was to serve as a simple multi-purpose utility aircraft. Work on the design began in 1963 and the prototype made its first flight on 13 June, 1965. Before the first flight of the production prototype on 20 August, 1966, it had been re-engined and had a 1.22m wingspan increase. Over the years of construction both at Bembridge on the Isle of Wight and later by Romaero in Romania due to the Isle of Wight plant being unable to keep up with initial demand, the company has produced over 1,250 aircraft. Many of these are still in service today, with around 500 operators in 120 countries, serving with both civil and military operators in such roles as air taxi, light freight, crop spraying and commuter operators in the commercial field. It also carries out various jobs in the military and marine domains. In fact, Britten Norman markets the aircraft as one that can be personalised to suit individual operator's needs.

The aircraft has had many variants over the years, with highest levels of production being in the mid-70s when the 500th airframe was delivered. There

FIRST FACTS	
Launched	1963
First Flight	13/06/65
Certification	08/67

has even been a single example re-engined with Dowty ducted fans.

The aircraft is still in production today, over 50 years after the prototype first took to the skies, with nearly 1,300 produced. The current standard model includes enlarged baggage bay door options, three-bladed scimitar propellers, low drag fairings, and a contemporary interior including ergonomically designed leather seats and on-board entertainment options. Production has also moved back to the UK.

STATS	
Length	10.86m (35ft 8in)
Height	4.18m (13ft 9in)
Wingspan	14.94m (49ft)
Typical/Max seats	9/9
Number built	1,280

Airbus A350XWB

FIRST FACTS	-900	-1000
Launched	01/12/06	01/12/06
First Flight	14/06/13	24/11/16
Certification	30/09/14	21/11/17
First Delivery	22/12/14 Qatar Airways	20/02/18 Qatar Airways
Entered Service	15/01/15 Qatar Airways	24/02/18 Qatar Airways

Following on from the announcement by Boeing about its new project the 787, Airbus initially looked at a re-engined and re-winged A330 to compete, although this was soon dropped in favour of an all-new design, albeit still similar to the A330. In the following two years and in response to feedback from many industry leaders, the design further evolved and was again re-designed into what we see today, most notable the extra width to the fuselage, hence the XWB addition to the title which stands for extra wide body. This extra width allowed the possibility of seating 10 abreast in a high-density configuration, enabling 440 or 475 seats depending on the variant. This brand-new aircraft was officially given the go ahead on 1 December, 2006. Given

the complexities of this technologically advanced aircraft, there were some initial challenges which resulted in increases in development costs and slippages in the programme, delaying both first flights and first deliveries to early customers Qatar Airways and Singapore Airlines. Airbus had originally seen a market for three versions; however, the shortest of these, the -800, was dropped in mid-2014, leaving just the -900 and -1000 available for sale. The financial outlay to Airbus was quite significant and came at a time when the company was dealing with the challenges in the A380 program, so it was possibly a brave decision to go ahead at all.

But push ahead they did, and with orders increasing a brand-new, purpose-built assembly building was constructed at the main Toulouse site as well as another brand-new building at the Broughton plant in North Wales where the wings were to be produced.

On 14 June, 2013 the very first A350XWB, a -900, made its maiden flight. Following on from a five-aircraft flight test programme over 2,600 hours, the aircraft gained certification. This certification was as a variant of the A330-200, which meant airlines operating both types had greater flexibility when it came to flight crew, not to mention another selling point for Airbus!

The first aircraft was delivered to launch customer Qatar Airways on 22 December, 2014, with the aircraft making its entry into service on the Doha to Frankfurt route on 15 January the following year. In September the same year construction began on the stretched -1000 version, which subsequently made its first flight on 24 November, 2016. By this time, the aircraft was in service with 10 airlines.

Qatar Airways was again to be the recipient of the first aircraft and did so at a glitzy ceremony at the Toulouse delivery centre on 24 February, 2018, with the aircraft itself becoming the backdrop for a fantastic sound and light display. The following day it took off for its new home in Doha, performing flypasts of both the airport and the Doha City skyline and it was finally greeted with the traditional water arch provided by the Doha Airport fire crews.

On 28 April, 2018 the A350ULR (ultralong range) took to the skies for the first time, and, following its delivery to launch customer Singapore Airlines, made a return to serving the longest scheduled route in the world, Singapore Changi to New York Newark. This had previously been flown by an Airbus when Singapore Airlines operated an A340-500 on the same route. As at June 2018, Airbus had orders for 882 aircraft, of which 182 had been delivered to 17 different operators around the globe.

STATS	-900	-1000
Length	66.89m (219ft 6in)	73.88m (242ft 5in)
Height	17.05m (55ft 12in)	17.08m (56ft 1in)
Wingspan	64.75m (212ft 6in)	64.75m (212ft 6in)
Typical seats	325	366
Number Ordered (01/19)	724	170

Tupolev TU104

FIRST FACTS	104/A	104B
Launched	1953	N/A
First Flight	17/06/55	N/A
First Delivery	N/A Aeroflot	N/A Aeroflot
Entered Service	09/56 Aeroflot	N/A Aeroflot

Based on the Soviet Strategic Bomber the TU104 'Badger', the TU104 was the Soviet's first and the world's second jet airliner to enter service when it started flying with Aeroflot in 1956. Seating 50 passengers, this aircraft was first considered at the start of the 1950s but flew for the first time on 17 June, 1955. It was considered quite a handful to fly and the 16 aircraft lost in accidents is testament to this.

Just 20 airframes of the initial version were produced from the 201 built in total. The TU104A had more powerful engines, and through a redesigned cabin carried 70 passengers in two classes. It was introduced in 1958. The following year the slightly stretched 104B came into use, seating 100. The only other operator of the type was CSA of Czechoslovakia, who operated six of the 'A' version. The aircraft deploy a parachute on landing to enable it to operate at airports where the runways would not have been long enough otherwise.

Following retirement by Aeroflot, many aircraft were transferred to the Soviet military; however, a further accident caused them to permanently retire the type in 1981.

STATS	104/A	104B
Length	38.85m (125ft 6in)	40.05m (131ft 5in)
Height	11.90m (39ft 1in)	11.90m (39ft 1in)
Wingspan	34.54m (113ft 4in)	34.54m (113ft 4in)
Typical seats	50/70	1

de Havilland DHC-8

FIRST FACTS	-100	-200	-300	-400/Q400
First Flight	20/06/83	31/01/95	15/05/87	31/01/98
Certification	N/A	N/A	02/89	06/99
First Delivery	N/A	19/04/95	02/89	07/02/00
	N/A	BPX Colombia	Time Air	SAS
Entered service	23/10/84	N/A	N/A	N/A
	NorOntair	N/A	N/A	N/A

The Dash 8 was solely a de Havilland product as it had been designed and flown before the Bombardier takeover. It followed on from the not-so-successful DHC-7, although this time it had just two engines and didn't concentrate on STOL performance which meant it had a much wider customer potential.

Initially, the aircraft was to seat 36-39, and the prototype -100 version first took to the skies on 20 June, 1983. Following certification it entered service with NorOntair on 23 October, 1984. Modifications and stretches created three further variants: the -200 with a higher all-up weight and more powerful engines, the -300, stretched to take 50 seats, which made its first flight in May 1987, and the last, the -400, first flying in January 1988.

The -400 version of the aircraft became known as the Q400 in 1997 after modifications to decrease cabin noise levels through active noise suppression. It is now the only version still in production and following further modifications is now known as the Q400 NextGen, seating up to 90 passengers.

The Dash 8 order book is a much better read for the manufacturers than the Dash 7, having sold nearly 1,300 as of June 2018, to customers as diverse as Air Greenland in the far north through Luxair and SAS in Europe to QANTASLink and SAA Express in the southern hemisphere. On 8 November, 2018 Bombardier disclosed that it was selling the programme to the holding company of Viking Air, which already markets and manufactures the revived DHC-6 and DHC-2.

STATS	-100	-200	-300	-400/Q400
Length	22.25m (73ft)	22.25m (73ft)	25.70m (84ft 3in)	32.80m (107ft 8in)
Height	7.49m (24ft 7in)	7.49m (24ft 7in)	7.49m (24ft 7in)	8.40m (27ft 5in)
Wingspan	25.63m (84ft 11in)	25.63m (84ft 11in)	27.40m (90ft)	28.40m (93ft 2in)
Typical/Max seats	37/40	37/40	50/56	82/90
Total ordered (12/18)	299	105	267	638

Aviation Traders ATL.98 Carvair

LEWIS GRANT

Freddie Laker's Channel Air Bridge transported cars and passengers from Britain to mainland Europe but needed a replacement for its fleet of Bristol freighters as the capacity was insufficient. Laker also owned the aviation engineering firm Aviation Traders, but as developing an entirely new design was too expensive he used the company to convert the relatively inexpensive and readily available DC4s to do the job. The conversion required the whole of the fuselage forward of the wing to be replaced with a lengthened fuselage and bulbous nose section, with the flight deck being moved above a sideways hinged nose door which enabled 5 cars and 23 passengers to be loaded. The aircraft gained its name from its purpose, which was CAR Via AIR. A former World Airways C54 was the first conversion to fly on 21 June, 1961, with Channel Air Bridge starting services from Southend to Rotterdam in March 1962. A merger with Silver City Airways formed British United Air Ferries, which meant that this latter airline took delivery of 11 of the total 21 conversions. Other original operators were Intercontinental/Interocean, Ansett, Aviaco and Aer Lingus, who further modified the aircraft to carry horses or 55 passengers in a high-density design.

FIRST FACTS

First Flight	21/06/61
First Delivery	03/62 Channel Air Bridge
Entered Service	03/62 Channel Air Bridge

STATS

Length	31.27m (102ft 7in)
Height	9.09m (29ft 10in)
Wingspan	35.81m (117ft 6in)
Typical/Max seats	23/55
Number built	21

Hawker Siddeley HS.748

FIRST FACTS	1/2/2A	2B/SUPER
Launched	1957	N/A
First Flight	24/06/60	06/79
First Delivery	04/62	N/A
	Skyways-Coach Air	N/A

In 1957 Avro were becoming concerned about the potential lack of future defence spending and looked again to the commercial market. One of many designs aimed at replacing the DC3, the 748 was initially planned to be a 20-30 seater, but following feedback from potential customers this was increased to 40. Avro decided to produce quite a rugged design, which would be able to operate from smaller, less prepared airfields. In addition, it was designed to be easy to repair and required little in the way of ground equipment. The design proved very popular with airlines around the world and orders were soon being placed.

The 748 was manufactured at the Woodford site not far from Manchester Airport, and it was from there that the aircraft first took to the skies on 24 June, 1960 with Skyways-Coach Air taking the first delivery in April 1962. In 1967 the first series 2 aircraft were being produced, having first flown in that September, and Avro had been fully absorbed into Hawker Siddeley. This new version had an increased gross weight and had more powerful Dart Mk531 engines. A series of improvements such as a large freight door, even more powerful engines, larger wing, better cabin layouts and an advanced flight deck saw the 748 through a number of series designations right through to the Super 748 in 1984 when the company was now BAe.

Howard Hughes apparently made a number of flights in the aircraft despite not having flown for 13 years.

In India 89 aircraft were assembled under licence by Hindustan Aeronautics, all of which were for Indian operators. The aircraft was also modified into a specialised military transport aircraft designated the HS.789 Andover. This aircraft was able to kneel down at the rear, enabling cargo to be loaded through clamshell doors with the use of a ramp.

In later years many aircraft found use as both combi and pure freight aircraft and many are still in use today. In total 380 had been constructed by the time the last aircraft left the factory in January 1989. As an aside, the factory and airfield itself has also now ceased to exist, having been demolished to make way for housing in 2017.

STATS	1/2/2A	2B/SUPER
Length	20.42m (67ft)	20.42m (67ft)
Height	7.75m (24ft 10in)	7.75m (24ft 10in)
Wingspan	30.02m (98ft 6in)	31.23m (102ft 6in)
Typical/max seats	44/58	44/58
Number built	24/111/157	28/8 HS.780 31 HAL 89

Vickers VC10

FIRST FACTS	STD	SUPER
Launched	00/10/52	N/A
Rolled out	15/04/62	N/A
First Flight	29/06/62	07/05/64
Certification	23/04/64	N/A
Entered service	30/04/64 BOAC	01/04/65 BOAC

The VC10 was the last of the Vickers-built designs, but unfortunately it came a little too late as the 707 and DC8 were already well established, and meddling by the launch customer BOAC further hampered its attractiveness to other airlines despite being loved by the small number of both crew and passengers who flew it.

The aircraft's original design was constrained by BOAC for use on its routes to the Far East and Africa, requiring a 'hot and high' spec. This was achieved by Vickers but only by restricting payload, and therefore the operating economics were not that attractive. It was a particularly striking aircraft with a high T-tail and rear-mounted engines that created a quiet cabin. BOAC ordered 35 plus 20 options in May 1957, but constant design changes by the airline eventually resulted in just 29 of all versions being delivered.

The prototype aircraft made its maiden flight on 29 June, 1962, and the first production model flew on 8 November. The VC10 saw its first service with BOAC on 30 April, 1964. The only other operators to buy the aircraft from new were Ghana Airways and British United. Early on in the development process there were studies made into creating a higher capacity version, which resulted in a stretch of 3.96m (13ft) enabling an extra 23 passengers to be carried. This created a far superior aircraft with good operating economics but sadly it was all too late. The first Super VC10 flew on 7 May, 1964, just

eight days after the standard entered service, but while Boeing and Douglas were snapping up orders from around the world the only other airline to order the Super VC10 apart from BA was East African Airways, but they were subsequently repossessed when the airline ceased trading in 1977.

The vast majority of both the standard and super VC10s ended their days with the RAF as tanker/transports serving the UK's armed forces well into the new millennium, with the last RAF flight taking place on 20 September, 2013, ending 51 years of continuous service.

STATS	STD	SUPER
Length	48.36m (158ft 8in)	52.32m (171ft 8in)
Height	12.04m (39ft 6in)	12.04m (39ft 6in)
Wingspan	44.55m (146ft 2in)	44.55m (146ft 2in)
Typical seats	109/151	139/174
Number built	32	22

JULY

Boeing 747SP

FIRST FACTS

Launched	1973
Rolled out	19/05/75
First Flight	04/07/75
Certification	04/02/76
First Delivery	05/03/76 Pan Am
Entered Service	04/76 Pan Am

The SP or special performance version of the 747 was designed as a result of a number of factors: Pan Am and Iran Air were wanting a large capacity aircraft for routes from the US to the Middle East, and Boeing themselves were also looking for an aircraft to compete with the DC10 and L-1011, whilst at the same time maintaining commonality with the existing 747s. In essence, there was a need for a longer-range 747 with fewer seats; therefore, Boeing simply shortened the existing 747-100/200 by 14.35m (47ft 1in) which enabled the aircraft to fly further and faster. There were other modifications required, most noticeably the enlarged vertical tail plane, but in essence it was a baby 747. Pan Am placed the launch order for 10 jets in 1973 and, following the first flight on 4 July, 1975, certification was achieved the following year. They received the first example on 5 March, 1976 named Clipper

Freedom. Unfortunately for Boeing, the aircraft did not sell too well, due mainly to the relatively poor operating economics. The SP was ordered by 13 airlines but most of the orders were for two or three, with only SAA ordering more at six. In later life the aircraft found new homes with the super rich, dignitaries and heads of state. In fact, Boeing actually opened up the SP production line five years after it was originally closed to produce one more aircraft for the United Arab Emirates, bringing the total produced to just 45. Possibly the most interesting operator is the highly modified SOFIA astronomical observatory, which has a sliding door in the rear fuselage allowing the use of a 2.5m diameter telescope to be operated above the majority of atmospheric conditions.

The aircraft set many distance records at the time, culminating in a world record 8,940nm (16,560km) non-stop delivery flight of an SAA aircraft from Paine field to Cape Town in 1976, a record only broken 13 years later by a 747-400.

STATS

Length	56.31m (184ft 9in)
Height	19.94m (65ft 5in)
Wingspan	59.64m (195ft 8in)
Typical/Max seats	276-316/440
Number built	45

Ilyushin IL18

Possibly one of the most enduring Soviet-built aircraft, the IL18 was designed to meet the needs of its principal user Aeroflot on their medium range routes, carrying 75-100 passengers. The aircraft was the first Soviet-built type to have an automatic approach system as well as the new weather radar.

The prototype aircraft took to the skies above Moscow on 4 July, 1957, with production aircraft soon following. The engines on these initial production aircraft proved so problematic that only 20 were built to this standard before an improved version was introduced with improved engines and a higher gross weight. This version, the IL18B, first flew on 30 September, 1958. The IL18 was a huge success, and not only did it fly with Aeroflot and other Soviet bloc countries, but it also made it outside the iron curtain. In total it flew with 17 foreign operators, and some are actually still in service today. The number of aircraft built is unknown but estimated to be in excess of 700 and, as is often the case with Soviet-era aircraft, it had many versions including both civil and military, from fisheries to Polar operations, and communications to casevac.

FIRST FACTS

Launched	1954
Rolled out	06/57
First Flight	04/07/57
First Delivery	04/59 Aeroflot
Entered Service	04/59 Aeroflot

STATS

Length	35.89m (117ft 9in)
Height	10.16m (33ft 4in)
Wingspan	37.40m (122ft 8in)
Typical seats	B-84 V-111 D/E-122
Number built	700+

VFW 614

FIRST FACTS

Launched	1968
First Flight	14/07/71
First Delivery	08/75 Cimber
Entered Service	08/75 Cimber

Unfortunately, another poor seller, the VFW-614 is a particularly distinctive aircraft as its engines were mounted in pods fixed to the top of the wings by pylons. Proposed as early as the 1960s, it was probably a little before its time, with the regional jet boom not really taking hold until the arrival of the Canadair CRJ in the early 90s. It was, however, the first jet-powered passenger airliner developed and built in Germany. Yet another DC3 replacement, it was built by a merged VFW and Fokker in the 1970s with the majority of the funding coming from the West German government and therefore another early multinational aircraft programme. The first prototype took to the skies on 14 July, 1971. Despite an aggressive marketing campaign, it did not gain many orders, partly due to a rather lengthy development programme – a situation made worse by the bankruptcy of Rolls Royce,

whose engines powered the new design, and the loss of the first prototype in an accident in 1972. The marriage of VFW and Fokker was also not a happy one with the two partners more often at loggerheads than working as a team.

Lufthansa were an obvious target for the aircraft, but having declined to purchase any this was another blow to the project, and by early 1975 there were just 10 on order and a total of 19 by the time the last aircraft flew in 1978. Operators were Cimber Air of Denmark who received the first of five production aircraft in August 1975 after the first flight four months earlier. Air Alsace and Touraine Air Transport were the only other airline operators, and the Luftwaffe the only other operator from new. In fact, of the 19 built 13 were delivered three others flew but were never delivered and the others were dismantled.

STATS

Length	20.60m (67ft 7in)
Height	7.82m (25ft 8in)
Wingspan	21.50m (70ft 7in)
Typical/Max seats	40/44
Number built	19

Vickers Viscount

FIRST FACTS	630	700/D	800	810
Launched	09/03/46	N/A	1952	N/A
First order	None	08/52	1953	N/A
First Flight	16/07/48	28/08/50	29/09/56	23/12/57
Certification	27/07/50	N/A	N/A	N/A
First Delivery	None N/A	04/53 BEA	02/57 BEA	N/A Continental
Entered service	N/A BEA	04/53 BEA	02/57 Continental	05/58

Developed in tandem with Rolls Royce's development of their Dart engine, the world's first commercially successful gas turbine prop engine, the Viscount, was born from the British government's Brabazon Committee, which was set up to look at the requirements of post-war transport aircraft. A number of designs made it to the skies but none were as commercially successful as the Viscount. Yet another potential DC3 replacement, the first of two prototypes flew on 16 July, 1948, although it was later that the Dart was incorporated and with the extra power these brought the seating capacity was increased to 53, which made the aircraft a lot more interesting to the airlines as it

had much better operating costs and a previously reticent BEA ordered 27 shortly after this version's first flight on 28 August, 1950. This set in motion what was to become Britain's most commercially successful airliner and the first turboprop airliner to enter production.

This new version, the V.700, had a stretched fuselage to allow for these extra passengers as well as an increased wingspan. BEA put the aircraft into service in April 1953, with airlines from all over the globe placing orders from TAA in Australia to Trans Canada bringing the aircraft to North America. Passengers loved the aircraft, not only for its famous panoramic windows but also due to it being pressurised and having a reduction in vibration and noise over previous types.

Vickers continued to develop the aircraft and Rolls Royce also further developed the Dart engine to provide more power. This combined with more efficient props produced a greater cruising speed and increase in take-off weight. A considerable amount of the Vickers modifications that became standard in all aircraft came from requirements of a new customer and a new market, with Capital Airlines in the USA having ordered 60 throughout 1954. This version, the 700D, then garnered further orders from a multitude of customers like Braathens SAFE, MEA, Indian Airlines and Alitalia in addition to several military and corporate versions being produced. These orders helped this version to become the best-selling of all models, requiring two factories to keep up with the required production.

With Rolls Royce announcing an even more powerful version of the Dart in 1952, a stretched version, the V.800, was developed to seat up to 71 passengers, but it didn't turn out to be a fantastic

seller as some compromises on speed and payload performance had to be made. The final version was the V.810, which, thanks to even more powerful Darts, got over the previous difficulties. After making its first flight on 23 December, 1957, its launch customer Continental Airlines put the aircraft into service between Chicago and LA in May 1958. A high-profile list of customers followed, including Lufthansa, PIA, SAA, Ansett and All Nippon. The last of 444 viscounts of all versions was delivered to China's CAAC in 1964, ending 12 years of production of this popular airliner.

STATS	630	700/D	800	810
Length	22.71m (74ft 6in)	24.74m (81ft 2in)	25.91m (85ft)	25.91m (85ft)
Height	8.15m (26ft 9in)	8.15m (26ft 9in)	8.15m (26ft 9in)	8.15m (26ft 9in)
Wingspan	N/A	28.56m (93ft 9in)	28.56m (93ft 9in)	28.56m (93ft 9in)
Typical/Max seats	32/32	40/63	52/71	52/71
Total No ordered	2 prototype	138/150	68	86

de Havilland Comet

FIRST FACTS	1/2	4	4B	4C
Launched	1943	N/A	N/A	N/A
First Flight	27/07/49	28/08/50	27/06/59	31/10/59
First Delivery	01/51 BOAC	04/53 BEA	04/60 BEA	01/60 Mexicana
Entered service	02/05/52 BOAC	04/53 BEA	04/60 BEA	01/60 Mexicana

Another design to come out of the Brabazon committee recommendations, the Comet was the first jet airliner and perhaps one of the most important aircraft ever produced. However, this same first almost certainly led to its lack of commercial success.

The Brabazon type IV recommendation was for a pressurised, jet-powered mailplane that could cross the Atlantic (later to take 100 passengers). The initial design went through a number of changes due mainly to input from BOAC, a decision that caused this and other aircraft of the period to be rather too specific to one airline and thereby reducing the attractiveness to others. As the aircraft was highly advanced for its time and years ahead of the competition from manufacturers in the US, this could well have been rectified but there were problems lurking literally beneath the surface. In 1949 the first prototype was completed and after ground tests it made its first flight on 27 July, 1949 from the Hatfield site in southern England. Soon after, it made its public debut at that year's Farnborough Airshow before starting the flight test programme.

The aircraft's all-metal skin was a thin alloy of a new design and needed to withstand being pressurised as well as flying at the speeds that the Comet's four jet engines produced, as well as the extremes of heat and cold it would encounter during its operation.

The launch customer, BOAC, put the aircraft into service on 2 May, 1952 with a service to Johannesburg; however, while the passengers were enjoying the quiet comfort of the aircraft's cabin, the crew flying were becoming increasingly concerned with a number of issues. Pilots reported that the aircraft had faulty seals in the new hydraulic system that required them to carry hydraulic fluid to keep the system topped up. The navigation system and some electrical systems were also reported to sometimes overheat and the cockpit windows could mist up. More importantly though was the report that the feedback from the control column felt the same no matter what speed the aircraft was flying at, and this led to a feeling that the aircraft was at least a handful to operate if not a little dangerous. Unfortunately, these fears were realised when an aircraft ran off the end of the runway in Rome in October 1952. Fortunately, there were no injuries but the aircraft was written off. Even though the cause was said to be pilot error as he raised the nose too much on take off, thereby increasing drag to the wings, it did bring to the fore this lack of feedback which was said to have allowed the nose to be raised too much. Unfortunately, just a few months later a similar incident occurred but this time all 11 crew on the training flight lost their lives when the aircraft hit a stone bridge in Karachi, which was followed by another incident shortly after which fortunately just led to aircraft damage.

There was worse to come. On 2 May, 1953 an aircraft broke apart during extreme turbulence, killing 43 on a flight from Delhi. Then in January 1954 the problems got much worse. Again departing Rome, communication with a BOAC flight was suddenly lost and witnesses saw burning debris falling from the skies following multiple explosions. Sales had been good to this point, with Air France and Union Aéromaritime de Transport having already received their aircraft with JAL, Panair do Brasil, Air India amongst others ordering the under-development Comet 2, and more significantly Capital Airlines, National Airlines and the mighty Pan Am having ordered the larger transatlantic Comet 3.

BOAC and Air France immediately grounded the aircraft. Despite investigations leading to over 50 modifications, no single cause could be identified and by a small majority vote BOAC put the aircraft back into service. But on 8 April that same year another aircraft exploded in mid-air and both the aircraft and the whole project was grounded. Subsequent investigations revealed that the continuous pressurisation then depressurisation had caused the thin skin of the aircraft to crack at the corners of the square windows. The aircraft needed a complete redesign. This redesign allowed the rest of the airline industry to catch up and moreover to learn from de Havilland and their problems.

All Comet 1s were withdrawn from service and were scrapped or had oval windows installed and strengthening modifications incorporated. Comet 2s in production were also modified, but these only ever went to the RAF as all airlines cancelled orders for this and the Comet 3, the latter making its first flight in July 1954. This aircraft was used in development flying and route proving for the much larger, longer range and ultimately much more successful Comet 4. Cancelled orders of the Comet 3 were transferred to the Comet 4, and BOAC was again the launch customer placing an order for 15 in March 1955. Flying for the first time on 27 April, 1958 and receiving its certification six months later, BOAC restarted commercial Comet operations the following day. The Comet still managed the accolade of being the first aircraft to operate regular transatlantic jet services when, on 4 October, 1958, BOAC started its service from London to New York. Only two other airlines ordered the Comet 4 – Aerolineas Argentinas and East African Airways. However, further versions were ordered by other airlines. The slightly stretched 4B that first flew on 27 June, 1959 was ordered by Olympic. The 4C, which had increased range and extra seats, was ordered by Kuwait Airways, MEA, Misrair and Sudan Airways after making its first flight on 31 October, 1959 and entered service with Mexicana the following year, making it the most popular variant. Comets found their way into secondary service with many airlines once they were superseded by newer jets, Dan Air being the most significant operator flying nearly 50 examples right into the 1980s,

STATS	1/2	4	4B	4C
Length	28.35m (93ft)	33.99m (111ft 6in)	35.97m (107ft 10in)	35.97m (118ft)
Height	8.65m (28ft 5in)	8.99m (29ft 6in)	8.99m (29ft 6in)	8.99m (29ft 6in)
Wingspan	35.05m (115ft)	35.00m (114ft 10in)	32.87m (93ft 9in)	35.00m (114ft 10in)
Typical/Max seats	36/44	74/106	101/119	101/119
Total No ordered	37	29	18	30

Embraer EMB120 Brasilia

Design work on this Brazilian twin turboprop passenger and cargo transport commenced in late 1979. Embraer were keen to follow on from the Bandeirante and to provide a larger aircraft for airlines looking to move up from its 19 seats. The first of three 30-seat prototypes first flew on 27 July, 1983 with certification following on 10 May, 1985. The launch customer came from Atlantic Southeast Airlines in North America; however, the major user came from closer to home – the Brazilian Air Force – along with Swiftair of Spain. 354 of this successful regional airliner have been produced.

FIRST FACTS

Launched	09/79
First Flight	27/07/83
First Delivery	06/85 Atlantic Southeast Airlines
Entered Service	10/85 Atlantic Southeast Airlines

STATS

Length	20.00m (65ft 8in)
Height	6.35m (20ft 10in)
Wingspan	19.78m (64ft 11in)
Typical seats	30
Number built	354

Tupolev TU134

FIRST FACTS	134	134A
Launched	10/62	1968
First Flight	29/07/63	22/04/69
First Delivery	09/67 Aeroflot	N/A Aeroflot
Entered Service	09/67 Aeroflot	09/11/70 Aeroflot

The easily recognisable Soviet airliner had initially started as an upgrade to the TU124, but once it emerged from the factory it had become an all-new design in the same style as similar-sized current western airliners the DC9 and BAC1-11, with all three having a T-tail and two rear-mounted engines. However, this is where, unlike other Soviet designs, the similarity ended. Its thin and angular style and swept back wings and tail planes gave it a unique look, particularly with the initial versions having a glass nose. The first TU134 took to the skies on 29 July, 1963, with Aeroflot taking the first delivery in September and putting the aircraft into service in the same month.

Tupolev introduced an uprated 134A with improvements to the avionics and more powerful engines and the introduction of weather radar, which meant that the nose now lost its traditional glazed finish. It entered service in 1970. This version also did away with the need for a parachute braking system. The 'Crusty', as NATO designated it, went on to become one of the most widely used in Soviet countries. The 134 was the first Soviet airliner to receive international certification from ICAO. Aeroflot and the Soviet Air Force were by far the biggest users, but Tupolev received export orders from a number of airlines including Interflug, LOT and CSA. Of the 854 built, a considerable number went on to have long and productive lives with secondary airlines as well as conversions to VIP transports. Although numbers are dwindling, there are still a number in use today.

STATS	134	134A
Length	34.34m (112ft 8in)	37.05m (121ft 7in)
Height	9.14m (30ft)	9.14m (30ft)
Wingspan	29m (95ft 2in)	29m (95ft 2in)
Typical/Max seats	64/72	84/96

AUGUST

BAe ATP

FIRST FACTS

Launched	01/04/84
First Flight	06/08/86
Certification	03/88
First Delivery	1988 BMA
Entered Service	09/05/88 BMA

Retaining the cross section of its predecessor the HS Super 748, but with a 5.03m (16ft 6in) stretch, the ATP was designed as a follow on from it and was aimed at the market for short-range, fuel efficient and low noise turboprop aircraft. Although this was certainly an important and thriving market sector, the ATP was possibly a little too late because by the time it entered the marketplace it was having to compete with well-established designs from ATR and de Havilland.

The ATP was designed to carry up to 72 passengers and was considerably upgraded throughout, with an EFIS cockpit, and slow-turning, six-bladed props attached to new generation PW engines. The aircraft first took to the skies from the BAe plant at Woodford in Cheshire on 6 August, 1986, and after certification was received in

March 1988. The launch customer, BMA, took the first production aircraft (G-BMYM) and inaugurated revenue service in May 1988.

The ATP's late entry into the market was probably the single biggest factor in its slow sales. Only 64 were ever built, and, despite an attempt to generate new sales by rebranding the aircraft the Jetstream 61 in 1995, no further aircraft were sold and the two aircraft built as J61 were scrapped, as were a number of ATP fuselages. The 64 aircraft that were sold were spread around a number of different customers, with the likes of BA, Loganair, Manx, Biman Bangladesh, SATA and United Express/Air Wisconsin, the latter being the only US operator of the type.

The aircraft has found a new lease of life more recently with a freighter conversion programme spearheaded, in conjunction with BAE, by West Air of Sweden, who now operate 15.

STATS

Length	26.01m (85ft 4in)
Height	7.59m (24ft 11in)
Wingspan	30.63m (100ft 6in)
Typical/Max seats	64/72
Number built	64

Embraer ERJ135/145

FIRST FACTS	145	135
Launched	12/06/89	16/09/97
First Flight	11/08/95	04/07/98
Certification	10/12/96	06/99
First Delivery	19/12/96 Continental Express	23/07/99 Continental Express

Originally based around the fuselage of the EMB120 and with a first flight originally expected sometime in 1991, the 145 project was considerably delayed by difficulties at Embraer and resultant cutbacks. However, the company pulled through and around the time of the initial expected first flight an all-new design had been agreed, with just the Brasilias three abreast fuselage cross section being retained. It was produced in two versions, with a heavier and longer-range version, the LR, being certi-

fied in May 1998. The 145 seemed to do particularly well in the US where, in addition to Continental's 75 aircraft, AMR Eagle ordered 42. These numbers were further increased when, in September 1997, Embraer launched the ERJ135. This shortened version carried just 37 passengers (50 in the 145) and made its first flight on 4 July, 1998, with Continental Express again taking the first example. A considerable number are still in service today, flying with 36 airlines in 26 countries.

STATS	145	135
Length	29.87m (98ft in)	26.34 (86ft 5in)
Height	6.75m (22ft 2in)	6.75m (22ft 2in)
Wingspan	20.04m (65ft 9in)	20.04m (65ft 9in)
Typical seats	50	37
Number built	1,216 of all variants as of August 2018	

BAe/HS 125

Destined to become probably the most successful British commercial aircraft ever produced, with over 1,600 built, and the world's longest in-production business jet ever, the 125 has had many guises. Originally the de Havilland DH125 Jet Dragon, it became the HS 125 by the time the aircraft entered production. Later on, with Hawker Siddeley becoming part of British Aerospace, it was renamed the BAe 125 until that company sold the business jet division to Raytheon, at which point the Hawker name was resurrected and added to the current variant, creating the Hawker 800 and 1000.

The first prototype flew from Hatfield on 13 August, 1962, although production within the UK was done at Broughton near Chester at the site now occupied by Airbus until around the turn of the century, when sub-assemblies were being sent over from various UK plants to Wichita in the US for final assembly.

The 125 was one of the first generation of this new type of aircraft and was, and still is, operated by a wide range of customers, even with airlines, finding a particular niche in the USA. Quite a number of versions have been produced over the years in a bid to compete with newer and larger competitors, and it has also been used by the world's military in a variety of roles from trainer through to flight inspection and VIP transport.

FIRST FACTS

Launched	1961
First Flight	13/08/62
First Delivery	10/09/64

STATS

Length	15.39m (50ft 6in)
Height	5.26m (17ft 3in)
Wingspan	14.33m (47ft)
Typical/Max seats	8/14
Number built	1600+

Grumman Gulfstream 1

The actual designation for this aircraft was the G-159 and it was originally designed for use as a business aircraft, although many found their way into commuter airline use. In 1957 a design of a low-wing, cantilever monoplane with an aluminium alloy, semi-monocoque fuselage was fixed on. Powered by the popular Rolls Royce Dart engine, the first aircraft took off from New York on its maiden flight on 14 August, 1958.

Certification was awarded in May 1959 and deliveries of this multi-use aircraft began soon after. The aircraft was configured in whatever layout the customer required, which could be anything up to 24 for the initial versions, although Grumman produced a stretched version seating 37 for use by regional airlines, with the likes of American Eagle and Continental Express operating it via their partner airlines. It was also used by airlines in Europe, Africa and the Middle East. The aircraft also found its way into military service as well as government agencies and NASA. Possibly the most well-known operator was Disney, and this example is now on display at Disney's Hollywood Studios in Florida.

FIRST FACTS	
Launched	06/57
First Flight	14/08/58
Certification	02/05/59

STATS	
Length	19.43m (63ft 9in)
Height	6.93m (22ft 9in)
Wingspan	23.93m (78ft 6in)
Typical/Max seats	8/37
Number built	200

Bristol 175 Britannia

FIRST FACTS	100	300
Launched	07/48	N/A
First Flight	16/08/52	31/07/56
Certification	1955	N/A
First Delivery	30/12/55	N/A
	BOAC	N/A
Entered Service	01/02/57	N/A
	BOAC	N/A

Designed to meet a BOAC requirement to transport 90 passengers across the Atlantic, the Bristol Britannia was a medium to long-range, four-engined turboprop first thought about during the Second World War. It was another airframe to come from the Brabazon committee recommendations of 1943. The same failings of the UK aircraft procurement systems that dealt blows to the likes of the Comet, Trident and VC10 dealt a blow to the Britannia, with many re-designs rendering the aircraft with limited appeal other than to BOAC, the instigator of these re-designs. With the jet age just around the corner, this meant that once the design had evolved into something with greater appeal the age of the turboprop was on the wane.

The prototype first flew from Filton on 16 August, 1952. The flight was far from uneventful, with the controls reported to be 'over sensitive' and an undercarriage issue that was only just fixed in time for landing but which filled the cockpit with smoke. Flight testing did not go to plan either, with the loss of one of the flight-test aircraft following an engine fire and subsequent forced landing. Additionally, there were engine icing issues requiring further and significant development, which lead to delays in certification and in turn delivery to launch customer BOAC, who put it into service in February 1957. These engine icing issues plagued the aircraft throughout its operational life.

Initial versions seated just 48, but a number of variants increased this number to 139. The series

300 first flew on 31 July, 1956. The majority of operators of the Whispering Giant, as it became known, were UK-based but orders came from Mexico, Cuba, Ghana and Canada.

In Canada, a piston-engined derivative of the Britannia, the Canadair Argus, served in the maritime patrol role. Tyne-powered stretched developments of the Britannia were also produced there as the Canadair Yukon for RCAF transport use and as the Canadair CL-44D, which was fitted with a swing-tail and used for freight operations.

STATS	100	300
Length	35.00m (114ft)	37.88m (124ft 3in)
Height	11.43m (37ft 6in	11.43m (37ft 6in)
Wingspan	43.36m (142ft 3in)	43.36m (142ft 3in)
Typical/Max seats	81/90	139/139
Number built	85 across all variants	

de Havilland DHC-2 Beaver

FIRST FACTS

Launched	17/09/46
First Flight	16/08/47
First Delivery	04/48 Ontario Dept of Lands and Forests

The design for this rugged, STOL utility aircraft came not from an airline's requirements or aerodynamic or financial constraints, but it was broadly based on the requirements of a number of Canadian bush pilots. It is said that in response to de Havilland telling them that their requirements would lead to poor flight performance, the response was 'you only need to be faster than a dog-sled to be a winner'. The aircraft was aimed at Canada's wild north and to operate in all seasons and most weather conditions. It could be equipped with wheels, skis or floats to transport its passengers and cargo in a range of operating conditions to remote areas using unprepared strips or lakes. Given the expected cold climate it was to operate in, the design even incorporated a system whereby the oil reservoir could be filled in flight from the cockpit. In 1987 the Canadian Engineering Centennial Board named the DHC-2 as one of the top-10 Canadian engineering achievements of the 20th century, and aviation publication Plane & Pilot described the type as being 'arguably the best bush plane ever built'.

The prototype made its maiden flight from de Havilland's Downsview factory on 16 August,

1947, and after a number of modifications and adjustments the first production model was delivered to the Ontario Department of Lands and Forests in April 1948.

Surprisingly, given this aircraft's now iconic status and sales record, initial sales were slow. However, fate was to play a hand, and with the US Army ordering it as its new utility aircraft just before the outbreak of the Korean War this led to many more sales, with a total of 970 ultimately being delivered. The aircraft quickly gained sales all around the world due to its capabilities and design, serving with many nation's military as well as in roles such as crop dusting, air taxi, sightseeing and police and border forces, in addition to more general civil aviation duties.

Over 1,600 of the aircraft were built and hundreds are still in use today, increasingly within the leisure industry in areas such as sightseeing and skydiving. In fact, the current owner of the type certificate, Viking, has mooted a return to production, although currently the only 'new' Turbo Beavers are existing airframes that have been rebuilt.

STATS

Length	9.22m (30ft 3in)
Height	2.74m (9ft)
Wingspan	14.63m (48ft)
Typical seats	6
Number built	1,632

BAC 1-11

FIRST FACTS	200/300/400	500
Launched	09/05/61	01/67
Rolled out	28/07/63	N/A
First Flight	20/08/63	30/06/67
First Delivery	09/04/65 BUA	08/68 BEA
Entered Service	09/67 BUA	N/A BEA

The origins of the 1-11 go back as far as the 1950s when Vickers Armstrong and Hunting were working on separate design studies for a short-haul aircraft. The aircraft that eventually made it into production stemmed from the Hunting design, the H107, although studies showed that this 59-seat aircraft was going to be too small and the design was modified into an 80-seater. Fortunately, the UK aviation industry seemed to have learnt from its previous mistakes and designed the aircraft for the industry as a whole and not one carrier. By the time of the first flight on 20 August, 1963 the order book was already looking very positive, not only in numbers but geographically as well, with orders from Braniff, Mohawk and most notably American Airlines in the USA in addition to launch

customer British United. In fact, 60 orders for the 1-11-200 had been placed from around the world by the time of the aircraft's roll-out at Hurn. BAC announced two further versions in May of 1963 – the 300 and 400 – which had more powerful engines and therefore increased range. The 400 was the US version. The programme suffered a setback later that year on 22 October, as during stall testing the prototype aircraft crashed. This incident led in part to the introduction of stick shakers and pushers as part of the aircraft's stall protection systems. Nearly two years after the first flight the aircraft received its certification, and launch customer British United took delivery of the very first production 1-11 on 22 January, 1965, putting the aircraft into service on 9 April that same year following weeks of route proving. Such was the demand for the aircraft that a second production line was established at Weybridge to help meet this.

In 1967 BAC introduced a stretched 119-seat version – the series 500 – which became known as the Super One-Eleven, this aircraft taking to the skies for the first time on 30 June, 1967. Unfortunately, BAC slipped back into bad habits and due to allowing launch customer BEA to delay the aircraft whilst assessing its requirements, it allowed its US rivals the chance to make up lost ground and subsequently failed to sell the version in the US, with the DC9 and 737 sharing the spoils. BAC offered other versions of the aircraft in an attempt to compete with the likes of the F28 and to try and gain ground in different markets; however, these failed, and ultimately lead to the end of UK production. Major users of the aircraft, both new and secondary, included Court Line, Dan Air, British Caledonian, BEA/British Airways, European Aviation, Ryanair, Braniff, Florida Express, US Air, Austral and Okada Air.

The story does not end there, however, as production was moved to Romania. There had been

a plan in place for as many as 80 ROMBAC 1-11s to be built with reduced British content, including licence-built Spey engines, this aircraft being aimed at developing economies. The first flight took place on 18 September, 1982, with the first delivery being made to local flag carrier TAROM on 29 December the same year. Unfortunately, for a number of reasons, this project also failed to live up to expectations, with just nine aircraft being delivered. As of April 2018, there was just one aircraft remaining in service with Northrop Grumman as an avionics testbed.

STATS	200/300/400	500
Length	28.50m (93ft 6in)	32.61m (107ft)
Height	7.47m (24ft 6in)	7.47m (24ft 6in)
Wingspan	26.97m (88ft 6in)	28.50m (93ft 6in)
Typical/Max seats	65/89	97/119
Number built	58/9/70	86

Shorts SD330

FIRST FACTS

Launched	05/73
First Flight	22/08/74
Certification	18/02/76
First Delivery	06/76 Time Air
Entered Service	24/08/76 Time Air

The SD3-30, as it was originally designated, the 30 standing for 30 seats, was derived from the smaller Skyvan and retained many of its proven characteristics. The Skyvan was a STOL aircraft with a large square section, unpressurised fuselage with a low floor level and braced high-mounted wings with a twin-tail unit, and in many respects the SD330 looked very similar. The 'Shed', as it was affectionately known, was aimed at the burgeon-

ing regional or commuter airline market, and being a simple unpressurised design it was intended to be inexpensive to both buy and operate.

The project was given the go ahead in May 1973, with the first prototype taking to the skies on 22 August, 1974 and the first production model taking off on 15 December, 1975. Sales were initially slow, but as the aircraft built up a reputation as a rugged yet comfortable and quiet airliner, orders started to pick up, with regional operators like Henson Airlines, Golden West Airlines and Hawaiian Airlines in the US and DLT, Aer Lingus and Air UK in Europe. Sales were further buoyed by what became the definitive commercial version – the 330-200 – which had more powerful engines. The military used the aircraft in utility tactical transport roles such as paratroop deployment. In total, 141 of the aircraft were built.

STATS

Length	17.69m (58ft 1in)
Height	4.95m (16ft 3in)
Wingspan	22.76m (74ft 8in)
Typical seats	30
Number built	141

Aero Spacelines Guppy 201

Best known for its use by Airbus in the transportation of components around Europe, the Guppy family of outsize transport aircraft has its roots in the US space programme. The need to transport large sections of the Saturn IV rocket resulted in a Boeing 377 Stratocruiser being modified by increasing the rear fuselage section and replacing the upper fuselage with a bulbous outsize section. The whole tail section was detachable to enable loading. This aircraft first flew in September 1962 and was nicknamed the Pregnant Guppy.

The first Super Guppy, of which only one was built, was a modified C-97J StratoFreighter and first flew on 31 August, 1965. This was larger in every way and had the original piston engines replaced by turboprops. In March 1970 the Guppy-101 had an even larger lobe size with a taller fin and it was also the first to have a hinged nose to allow for straight in loading.

The most popular conversion was the Guppy 201. Four of these were built, two by UTA Industries in France, as this model was designed for the transportation of large airframe components. All were in use by Aeromaritime to transport the above mentioned Airbus components.

FIRST FACTS	
First Flight	24/08/70
First Delivery	1971 Airbus Industrie

STATS	
Length	43.84m (143ft 10in)
Height	14.78m (48ft 6in)
Wingspan	47.62m (156ft 3in)
Number built	4 (+1 Pregnant Guppy, 1 Super Guppy, 1 Mini Guppy and 1 Guppy 101)

The initial 201 flew for the first time on 24 August, 1970 and was used until 1998 when the last example was disposed of in favour of the A300-600ST Beluga.

All Guppies are still in existence today, with the majority in museums; however, one was still operational as late as 2017 with NASA, thereby completing a full circle.

Handley Page Herald

FIRST FACTS	
First Flight	25/08/55
First Delivery	05/61
	Jersey Air Ferries

Another of the intended DC3 replacements, the Herald was aimed more specifically at smaller airlines who suggested that a piston-powered aircraft was their preferred choice. This led to a design with four radial engines and it made its maiden flight on 25 August, 1955. However, despite the early interest, with the success of the turboprop-powered Viscount and Fokker making the same choice for its F27, it soon became clear that piston engines were the wrong decision and all orders were cancelled. Therefore, and not for the first time, a market lead for a British-built airliner was lost. The new design was named the HPR.7 Dart Herald and the original prototype, which was now stretched by 50.8cm (20in) allowing the forward crew baggage door to be clear of the props, and of course powered by just two Dart turboprops, made its first flight on 17 December, 1958. BEA made the first order in June 1959, but by then the F27 was already six months into service. Hawker Siddeley were soon to fly the 748 and therefore Handley Page needed to stimulate more

orders. A further stretch was made allowing for an increase in passengers to 56 from the original 44. This new -200 version flew for the first time on 8 April, 1961, with the first production aircraft being delivered to Jersey European Airlines in January 1962. However, the damage was done and just 50 of all variants were ever built. Many went on to find homes with secondary operators such as Air UK and British Air Ferries, who flew the last ever passenger service in 1987, with others continuing on as freighters.

STATS	200/400
Length	23.01m (75ft 6in)
Height	7.31m (24ft)
Wingspan	28.88m (94ft 9in)
Typical seats	56
Number built	50 across all variants

Fairchild Swearingen Metroliner

FIRST FACTS	I/II	III/23
First Flight	26/08/69	1981
Certification	06/70	N/A
First Delivery	1971 Air Wisconsin	N/A

This 19-seat regional turboprop can trace its lineage right back to the Swearingen Merlin executive aircraft of the mid-1960s, which itself then underwent a number of modifications and engine changes to become the SA226-T Merlin 111. The first aircraft to be named the Metroliner was a stretched version of this Merlin. Although able to seat 22 passengers, it was configured to seat 19 as this was the highest number of passengers allowed to be transported without the need for a Flight Attendant by the FAA. Work began in 1968 and on 26 August, 1969 the SA226-TC Metro took to the skies for the first time, with certification following on in June 1970. Delivery of the first aircraft to launch customer Air Wisconsin happened early in 1971; however, at around the same time Swearingen's financial difficulties became untenable and the programme was taken over by Fairchild, with

the Swearingen name being dropped. In 1974 Fairchild introduced the Metro II, which had rectangular windows in addition to improvements to the cabin. A more powerfully engined Metro III followed in 1981 – this aircraft also had an increased wingspan, modifications to wingtips, engine cowlings to reduce drag and four-bladed props. A further version named the Metro 23 (as it was designed for certification under FAR Part 23 regulations) was certified in June 1990, having a further increase in maximum take-off weight. Military and freight versions of this latter model were also offered. Of the over 1,000 aircraft of all versions produced, Metroliners have performed a number of tasks from counter narcotics reconnaissance in Colombia to the more regular commuter operations often in a fairly rugged environments like Australia, where the type has proven very popular.

STATS	I/II	III/23
Length	18.09m (59ft 4in)	18.09m (59ft 4in)
Height	5.08m (16ft 8in)	5.08m (16ft 8in)
Wingspan	14.10m (46ft 3in)	17.37m (57ft)
Typical/Max seats	19/22	19/22
Number built	Over 1,000 of all models	

McDonnell Douglas DC10

FIRST FACTS

Launched	02/68
First Flight	29/08/70
Certification	29/07/71
First Delivery	08/71 American Airlines
Entered Service	05/08/71 American Airlines

The DC10 was intended to be a replacement for Douglas's successful DC8 on long-haul routes. The design was intended to meet an American Airlines requirement which interestingly also led to the Lockheed Tristar. Seating up to 380 passengers, this three-engined jet was launched in February 1968 when American and United Airlines placed orders for the original DC10-10. The series 10 was intended for Domestic or US transcontinental use and flew for the first time on 29 August, 1970 and received its certification on 29 July, 1971, with American Airlines being the first to put it into service on 5 August, 1971. There were three other versions on offer from the manufacturer, with the -15 being the 'Hot and High' version with more powerful engines and a greater range. This version was ordered by Aeromexico and made its first flight in January 1981. The

-30 and -40 were even longer range international versions. The -30 was powered by General Electric engines and made its first flight in June 1972, with KLM and Swissair taking early deliveries, but the -40 had engines by Pratt and Whitney and was only ordered by Northwest and JAL – it made its first flight in February 1972, with the first delivery being made to Northwest. The DC10-30 was by far the most produced model and had variations itself including a convertible freighter version (-30CF), full freighter (-30F) and an extended range version (-30ER). The only visible difference between these later versions and the initial -10 was the addition of a central main undercarriage bogie.

The programme suffered a number of early setbacks that damaged the reputation of the aircraft as there were several accidents in the

1970s, initially because of difficulties with the cargo doors which had been designed as outward opening rather than the norm of inward. The most notable was Turkish Airlines Flight 981 that crashed on departure from Paris after a rear cargo door was not secured correctly and subsequently blew out, causing internal decompression that led to the severing of control cables, rendering the aircraft uncontrollable, with the loss of all 346 on board.

Further into the decade an American Airlines Flight 191 from Chicago to Los Angeles crashed immediately after take-off. The cause was eventually found to be an incorrect maintenance procedure. However, at the time this accident led to the FAA withdrawing the type's certificate on 6 June, 1979, which immediately grounded all US registered DC10s and the majority of non-US registered DC10s flying within the USA. Despite these and other incidents, McDonnell Douglas sold 386 of all commercial versions as well as 60 of the KC10 Extender Aerial refuelling tanker.

There are still a considerable number of aircraft still in service, although solely as freighters with FedEx being the largest operator. Many have undergone an MD10 conversion which has equipped the aircraft with an advanced two-crew EFIS flight deck.

STATS	
Length	55.50m (182ft 1in)
Height	17.70m (58ft 1in)
Wingspan	50.40m (165ft 5in)
Typical/Max seats	255/380
Number built	386 (+60 KC10)

Antonov AN2

FIRST FACTS

First Flight	31/08/47

This is possibly one of the most mass-produced aircraft ever, with something like 18,000 being built in three different countries with production still underway decades after the first flight. The AN 2 is the largest biplane still operating in the world today.

Following a Soviet Ministry of Forestry requirement, the aircraft was designed to be a tough and reliable workhorse with the ability to fly from just about any cleared piece of land, snow or water. The aircraft has excellent STOL capabilities and it is said that in the right conditions it is possible to 'hover' the aircraft or even fly backwards. This thirsty aircraft, which consumes around 2.5 litres of fuel per minute and has a NATO reporting name of 'Colt', has been used in a multitude of roles from water bombing to medevac and crop dusting to probably the most common – a 12-seater passenger version.

The first prototype, which had the designation SKh-1, flew for the first time on 31 August, 1947 with production models rolling out of the factory in Kiev from 1949. Reports vary widely as to numbers, but anything up to about 5,000 are said to have been produced there, with a further 13,000 in Poland by PZL, where the manufacture was transferred to in 1960. Furthermore, China have

been licence building the AN2 as the Y5 since 1957. Used extensively by ex-Soviet bloc airforces, it has seen action in a number of wars, the first being the Korean War in the early 1950s. On the civilian or commercial side, Aeroflot was of course a major operator, using the aircraft as a short-range airliner. There are still many thousands of the type working from anything as Canadian bush planes to regional airliners in developing countries as well as in the leisure industry, most notably as skydiving platforms.

STATS

Length	12.74m (41ft 10in)
Height	4.01m (13ft 2in)
Wingspan (Upper)	18.80m (59ft 8in)
Wingspan (Lower)	14.24m (46ft 9in)
Typical/Max seats	12/12
Number built	18,000+

Antonov AN 72/74

FIRST FACTS

First Flight	31/08/77

The An72/74 (NATO reporting name 'Coaler') was designed as a STOL transport aircraft intended to replace Aeroflots AN24s and the Soviet military's AN26s. Development on this unusual looking aircraft started in 1972 with the first of eight pre-series aircraft flying from Kiev on 31 August, 1977. However, it took over eight years before the first production model flew, this time from the Kharkov plant in December 1985, this transfer and design modifications causing the serious delay. The strange looking configuration of the aircraft with the engines mounted on top of the wings was, in fact, to increase its STOL capabilities by using what is known as the Coanda effect, which increases lift by blowing exhaust gasses over the wing's surface. Of these eight pre-series aircraft, two were designated AN74, which were specifically designed to operate in Polar regions for Aeroflot. The AN74 looked identical to the AN72 other than two blister windows at the rear of the flight deck and front of the cabin on the port side and the addition of a larger radome. Although mainly used in a variety of military capacities including the 'Madcap' AEW&C version, there were a number used as freighters (both full and combo) and executive transports.

STATS	
Length	28.07m (92ft 1in)
Height	8.65m (28ft 5in)
Wingspan	131.89m (104ft 8in)
Typical/Max seats	68/68
Number built	195

SEPTEMBER

Boeing 717

The MD95 was the only airliner to make it as a Boeing after the takeover over of McDonnell Douglas by Boeing in 1997. The latest in the DC9 family, it was formally launched as the MD95 in October 1995 with an order for 50 from Valujet in the US. It was specifically designed for the short-haul, high-frequency 100-passenger market. Relaunched as the 717-200 following the takeover, it took to the skies on 2 September, 1998, receiving its certification a year later. By the time of first delivery in September 1999, Valujet had become Air Tran. Indeed, it was Air Tran who took one of the two final 717s ever delivered in a ceremony before thousands of employees, retirees and dignitaries in Long Beach. These deliveries brought to an end commercial airline production at the plant that had started back in the 1920s. The 717 is still in use today with Airlines such as Volotea, Delta and QANTASLink.

FIRST FACTS

Launched	10/95
First Flight	02/09/98
Certification	1999
First Delivery	09/99 AirTran

STATS

Length	55.50m (182ft 1in)
Height	17.70m (58ft 1in)
Wingspan	50.40m (165ft 5in)
Typical/Max seats	106/117
Number built	156

BAe 146/RJ

FIRST FACTS	-100	-200	-300
First Flight	03/09/81	01/08/82	01/05/87
Certification	N/A	02/83	N/A
First Delivery	05/83 Dan Air	05/83 Air Wisconsin	12/88 Air Wisconsin
	RJ70/80	RJ85	RJ100
First Flight	23/06/92	23/03/92	13/05/92
First Delivery	N/A N/A	23/04/93 Crossair	07/93 THY

In August 1973 Hawker Siddeley, the forerunner of BAe, announced it was designing a four-engined, yet quiet, airliner. Recession and the oil crisis of 1974 led to this project being shelved, although work did not completely stop and in 1978 the project was relaunched and the resulting 146-100 made its first flight on 3 September, 1983. It was intended to fill the gap between turboprops like the company's 748 and the larger BAC1-11, as well as being simple to maintain and economic to operate. Certification was achieved on 8 February, 1983 and the first delivery was to Dan Air in May 1983.

Other users of this first variant were PSA and the Queen's Flight. A stretched version, the

-200, first took to the skies on 1 August, 1982. Seating another 10, the aircraft proved popular in the USA where it could operate into airfields previously not served by jets due to noise. Air Wisconsin took the first -200 in May 1983. The low noise footprint also led to the creation of the Quiet Trader (QT) which allowed it to operate into airfields at night. The 146-300 was a further stretch, and with the original -100 being modified to -300 standards, it flew for the first time on 1 May, 1987. Following certification, the first true -300 flew in June 1988 with deliveries again to Air Wisconsin beginning that December.

The upgraded RJs were first offered in 1990. The RJ70 and 80 were based on the 146-100, and

the RJ85 was based on the 146-200 and was the first to fly on 23 March, 1992 with first deliveries being made to Crossair of Switzerland. The RJ100 is based on the 146-300 and first flew on 13 May, 1992 operated by, in addition to launch customer Turkish, Ansett, Thai, China Northwest and SAM Colombia. All the RJs had an enhanced cabin, digital EFIS flight deck and avionics, and, whereas the 146s were built at Hatfield, the RJs were built at

Woodford near Manchester. Of the 387 of all variants built, there are still a considerable number in service today, although numbers are dwindling with the introduction of newer, more economical twin jets. All variants are one of a very small number of aircraft licensed to operate into London City Airport with its 5.5 degree glide-slope. A further version, the RJX, made it to prototype stage before the project was cancelled in November 2001.

STATS			
Length	26.19m (85ft 11in)	28.60m (93ft 10in)	30.99 (101ft 8in)
Height	8.61m (28ft 3in)	8.59m (28ft 2in)	8.59m (28ft 2in)
Wingspan	26.21m (86ft)	26.21m (86ft)	26.21m (86ft)
Typical/Max seats	70/94	80/112	100/128
Total No built	49	187	119

Beech 1900

In the late 1970s Beech came back to the regional airliner market. The largest of the new types was the 1900, a 19-seat pressurised turboprop based around a stretched King Air fuselage with a rear cargo door and a distinctive T-tail with added tail tip devices. The prototype made its maiden flight on 3 September, 1982 with certification achieved on 22 November, and deliveries were made to Bar Harbor Airlines in February 1984. Other operators included Continental, Mesa Airlines, Texas Air and Business Express.

In the early 1990s the 1900D replaced the basic 'C' version with the major differences being a raised roofline that made it easier to stand up in, more powerful engines, winglets and other aerodynamic devices. The new version took to the skies on 1 March, 1990, with Mesa Airlines taking delivery of the first of its 100 ordered in November that year. Beech also produced military and executive versions. As of July 2018, there were over 300 in service and two thirds of them are in the Americas.

FIRST FACTS

First Flight	03/09/82
Certification	22/11/83
First Delivery	02/84 Bar Harbor

STATS

Length	17.63m (57ft 10in)
Height	4.50m (14ft 11in)
Wingspan	16.60m (54ft 6in)
Typical/Max seats	19/19
Number built	695

Lockheed Jetstar

The Jetstar was originally designed for a USAF requirement that was ultimately cancelled; however, Lockheed persevered with the project, which eventually became the first dedicated biz jet to enter service. Taking to the skies for the first time on 4 September, 1957 this four-engined jet could carry up to 10 passengers 4,000km (2,500 miles). Although mainly used as executive transport, it has been used by airlines including Iraqi Airways, Eastern Airlines and TAESA. Possibly the most famous owner of a Jetstar was Elvis Presley, and his aircraft is now on display at Gracelands.

FIRST FACTS	
First Flight	04/09/57

STATS	
Length	18.41m (60ft 5in)
Height	6.22m (20ft 5in)
Wingspan	16.59m (54ft 5in)
Typical/Max seats	8/10
Number built	204

Britten Norman Trislander

Following on from the success of the Islander and market research suggesting there was a market for a higher capacity commuter airliner, Britten Norman stretched and modified the Islander to create the 18-seat, three-engined Trislander. After dumping a smaller stretch of the Islander, a prototype constructed from a prototype Islander first took to the skies on 11 September, 1970. Aurigney, who went on to become the major opera-

tor of the type, also had the honour of receiving the first aircraft in June 1971. The aircraft went on to find use with a number of airlines in the UK and USA in particular, but also with operators in the Pacific region and Africa. There have been attempts to get the aircraft back into production either from a number of kits built but never assembled or from new licence builds. Unfortunately, none of these attempts have produced any.

FIRST FACTS	
First Flight	11/09/70
Certification	05/71
First Delivery	06/71
	Aurigney

STATS	
Length	13.93m (45ft 8in)
Height	4.32m (14ft 2in)
Wingspan	16.15m (53ft)
Typical/Max seats	17/17
Number built	79

Airbus A220

FIRST FACTS	-100	-300
First Flight	16/09/13	27/02/15
Certification	18/12/15	11/07/16
First Delivery	29/06/16	28/11/16
Enter service	15/07/16 Swiss International	14/12/16 Air Baltic

The A220, although now officially an Airbus aircraft, was originally built by Bombardier as the C Series. In reality this aircraft is still built in Canada in the same factory at Montreal's Mirabell airport, although Airbus have started construction of a second production line at its Mobile Alabama facility. This medium-range, narrow-body airliner was first thought about back in 1998 when an expanded CRJ was evaluated. This project was never taken up and it was six years later that the Bombardier board started to look at a whole new commercial aircraft programme intended to replace ageing twinjets. The aircraft was to be in two sizes, carrying up to 115 passengers in the smaller

version and 135 in the larger in a 2/3 configuration. Although design work was all but put on hold for 2006, work restarted in 2007 with an official launch in July 2008 and a letter of intent from Lufthansa.

The programme went through a series of delays, but on 16 September, 2013 the smaller of the two, now with the designation of CS100, took to the skies over Montreal on its maiden flight. Unfortunately, the aircraft suffered more setbacks with delays to certification stemming from flight testing and an uncontained engine failure leading to the grounding of the aircraft.

Despite these difficulties, on 27 February, 2015 the CS300 made its first flight and certifica-

tion for the CS100 followed in December 2015. The first aircraft was delivered to Swiss International on 29 June, 2016. With type certification for the CS300 following the month after, the first of the larger variant was delivered to Air Baltic on 28 November, 2016.

After initially failing to agree a deal in 2015, Airbus and Bombardier formally agreed a partnership in which Airbus would have a majority stake in July of 2018. The aircraft at that time became the A220-100 and A220-300 for the CS100 and CS300 respectively.

STATS	-100	-300
Length	35.00m (114ft 9in)	38.70 (127ft)
Height	11.50m (37ft 8in)	11.50m (37ft 8in)
Wingspan	35.01m (115ft 1in)	35.01m (115ft 1in)
Typical/Max seats	108/133	130/160
Number ordered (01/19)	83	449

Airbus A320neo

FIRST FACTS	319	320	321	321LR
First Flight	31/03/17	25/09/14	09/02/16	31/01/18
Certification	21/12/18	19/12/14	15/12/16	N/A
First Delivery	None	20/01/16	05/17	13/11/18
	Lufthansa	Virgin America	Arkia	

Airbus had been working on improvements to enhance the A320's performance from as far back as 2006. The now standard sharklets and other aerodynamic refinements combined with weight savings were targeting a 5 per cent saving on fuel costs. In 2010 a now somewhat ironic order for the CS300 from Republic Airways Holdings, the owner of Frontier Airlines who, up to that point, had been an all Airbus operator, was the final push to re-engine the A320. A brand-new aircraft was simply not a financial option as any greater savings from a new airframe would not be enough to warrant the extra costs. Airbus state that the neo has an overall 15 per cent saving on fuel costs over the ceo, and for an investment expected to be around €1bn this was by far the best option, a decision that subsequently proved to be the right one, in fact, for both Airbus and their main competitor Boeing, who in turn were forced into

a re-engined 737, with both manufacturers selling in their thousands, despite problems with the supply of engines that led to wags stating Airbus were producing gliders.

The first of the new family took to French skies on 25 September, 2014 and was certified the following December. This much quieter aircraft was delivered to launch customer Lufthansa on 20

January, 2016. Next to fly was the A321neo on 9 February, 2016 and it achieved certification on 15 December, 2016, later than planned due to a tail strike early in the flight testing. Virgin America were the first recipient of this version, taking delivery from the Hamburg plant and putting it into service in May 2017. A further example of the A321neo, the A321LR (long range) first flew on 31 January, 2018. Initially, the launch customer was due to be Primera Air, but with their demise Arkia took the first aircraft on 13 November. Finally, the A319neo made its first flight on 31 March, 2017, achieving certification on 21 December that year. With the order book so light for the A318ceo, Airbus has no current plans to re-engine the smallest of their single-aisle family.

STATS	319	320	321	321LR
Length	33.84m (111ft)	37.57m (123ft 3in)	44.51m (146ft)	44.51m (146ft)
Height	11.76m (38ft 7in)	11.76m (38ft 7in)	11.76m (38ft 7in)	11.76m (38ft 7in)
Wingspan	35.80m (117ft 5in)	35.80m (117ft 5in)	35.80m (117ft 5in)	35.80m (117ft 5in)
Typical/Max seats	140/160	165/194	206/244	206/244
No. ordered (12/18)	55	4,191	6,526	inc in A321

Boeing 767

FIRST FACTS	-200/ER	-300/ER	-400ER
First Flight	26/09/81	30/01/86	09/10/99
Certification	30/07/82	22/09/86	N/A
First Delivery	19/08/82	1986	08/00
	United	JAL	Delta

The 767 was originally going to be a trijet, although it ended up as the medium-range twinjet we know today as it was developed alongside the 757. The initial base version, the -200, was launched with an order from United Airlines on 14 July, 1978. Boeing had originally intended to produce a smaller version but as it was close in capacity terms to the 757 this was not taken forward. Both types share a common EFIS flight deck operated by two crew. The 767 was offered with two engine options.

The 216-seat airliner took to the skies for the first time on 26 September, 1981 with initial type certification following in July. Launch customer United took delivery of the first aircraft (a Pratt and Whitney-engined model) on 19 August, 1982. Delta took the first GE powered aircraft on 25 October, 1982 and has since gone on to become one of the largest operators of the type. A longer-range version – the 200ER – made its maiden flight on 6 March, 1984, entering service with Ethiopian Airlines just a few weeks later on 23 May, 1984.

Boeing had been developing a stretched version since early 1982, with the extra 3.07m (10ft 1in) allowing, on average, an extra 50 passengers. Flying for the first time on 30 January, 1986, the

-300 entered service the following September with Japan Air Lines. As with the -200, an extended version of the 300 was developed with higher weights and greater fuel capacity, with this version taking to the skies on 19 December, 1986 and entering service with AA in February 1988, this version going on to be the bestseller with approximately 50 per cent of all non-military sales.

The 767 became the first wide-bodied Boeing jet airliner to receive two fuselage stretches when the final version – the 400ER – took to the skies on 9 October, 1999. There is also a freight version based on the -300 which found a number of operators, most notably UPS and DHL in addition to military tanker and AWACS versions.

STATS	-200/ER	-300/ER	-400ER
Length	48.51m (159ft 2in)	54.94m (180ft 3in)	61.30m (201ft 4in)
Height	15.85m (52ft)	15.85m (52ft)	16.80m (55ft 4in)
Wingspan	47.57m (156ft 1in)	47.57m (156ft 1in)	51.90m (170ft 4in)
Typical/Max seats	181/290	218/350	245/375
Total No built	128/121	104/583	38

Ilyushin IL96

FIRST FACTS	-300	M
First Flight	28/09/88	06/04/93
Certification	12/82	N/A
Entered service	1993 Aeroflot	N/A Aeroflot

The IL96's resemblance to the longer IL86 is superficial as it is a new design full of advanced technologies such as a six-screen EFIS flight deck and a fly-by-wire control system, and it is powered by new engines. Development started as far back as the mid-1980s with the first flight taking place on 28 September, 1988 and certification following in December 1982. It made its first entry into service with Aeroflot, the main user of the type, in early 1993. Ilyushin stretched the aircraft by 10m (30ft) and, aiming it at export sales, fitted it with western avionics and swapped the Russian engines for American Pratt and Whitney engines. This version was called the IL96M and the prototype made its first flight on 6 April, 1993, again entering service with Aeroflot. The IL96M was the first Russian-built aircraft to achieve US certification in June 1999. However, the only commercially operated IL96s still in service are the -300 version with Cubana.

STATS	-300	M
Length	55.35m (181ft 7in)	64.39 (211t 3in)
Height	17.57m (57ft 8in)	15.88m (52ft 1in)
Wingspan	60.10m (197ft 2in)	60.10m (197ft 2in)
Typical/Max seats	235/300	312/375
Number built	30	

OCTOBER

Tupolev TU154

FIRST FACTS	
Launched	1966
First Flight	04/10/68
First Delivery	1970 Aeroflot
Entered Service	05/71 Aeroflot

Announced in the spring of 1966, the TU154 was intended to replace the TU104, IL18 and AN10 on Aeroflot's medium to long sectors. The trijet was designed, like many of the Soviet aircraft of that era, to operate from poor unprepared strips and was aimed not only at Aeroflot but at the airlines in eastern Europe and China.

The first prototype took to the skies on 4 October, 1968 and entered service with Aeroflot in early

1970. It went on to become a mainstay of the fleet, carrying a substantial proportion of all Aeroflot's passengers during its heyday. Following the break up of the USSR, the type was seen in a myriad of colourful liveries from many of the former Soviet states, finding homes with many different airlines.

There have been many different versions of the aircraft, some stemming from initial problems found with early versions as well as the more normal route of higher gross weights and increasingly powerful engines. Initially seating up to 158 passengers, the latter versions could carry up to 180, although it remained the same size. The aircraft has also gone on to have many different roles from standard conversions such as freighters to monitoring aircraft and Buran cosmonaut training. It has also been used quite widely as government and military transport. There are very few aircraft known to remain in service, but the main stalwart of Soviet era aircraft, Air Koryo, is still thought to have two in its fleet.

STATS	
Length	47.90m (157ft 2in)
Height	11.40m (37ft 5in)
Wingspan	37.55m (123ft 3in)
Typical/Max seats	158/180
Number built	1026

Boeing 747-300

The -300 saw the first increase in cabin area for the 747 programme when Boeing increased the size of the famous hump after discounting any form of stretch to the fuselage. First called the SUD for stretched upper deck, this then became the EUD, replacing stretched with extended, and finally the -300. Flying for the first time on 5 October, 1982, this new version carried up to 20 extra passengers in the 7.11m (23ft 4in) longer upper deck, although a variant of the type – the 300SR – was produced as a high-density, short-range version. JAL operated this version with over 600 seats. Launch customer Swissair accepted delivery of the first aircraft on 23 March, 1983. This model did not sell in great numbers as it was soon superseded by the more advanced -400, but it saw service with the likes of Cathay Pacific, Egypt Air, KLM and SIA, amongst others, with some still in use with Saudia and JAL, and some modified versions being used as freighters.

FIRST FACTS

First Flight	05/10/82
First Delivery	23/03/83 Swissair

STATS

Length	70.66m (231ft 10in)
Height	19.33m (63ft 5in)
Wingspan	59.64m (195ft 8in)
Typical/Max seats	400/600
Number built	81

McDonnell Douglas MD80

FIRST FACTS	(GENERIC MD80)
Launched	00/10/77
First Flight	18/10/79
Certification	26/08/80
First Delivery	12/09/80 Swissair

Originally designated the DC9-80 or Super 80, this aircraft was developed as a stretch to the successful DC9 range of aircraft but with new engines and wings. Renamed as the MD80 (a generic term for all variants) in 1983, the aircraft made its first flight on 18 October, 1979 and received certification on 26 August, 1980, with first deliveries going to Swissair from 12 September, 1980. The next version was the MD82, which had an increased payload and range and was optimised for 'hot and high' performance. This took to the skies on 8 January, 1981. Certified on 31 July that same year, the first delivery was to Republic Airlines in August; however, it was American Airlines that went on to, in effect, both save the programme with their

initial order of 67, which kickstarted sluggish sales elsewhere, and become the largest operator of the type, acquiring 260 of all variants, just over 21 per cent of the total built of 1,191. An extended range model – the MD83 – first flew on 17 December, 1984, with Alaska Airlines and Finnair taking the first deliveries. Next came the MD87, which was the only version that was different in size to all the others. At 5.31m (17ft 5in) shorter than its stablemates, the MD87 was the first of the series to have an EFIS cockpit in addition to offering an optional head up display (HUD). The prototype flew for the first time on 4 December, 1986, and, following certification in October the following year, launch customers Austrian and Finnair received their aircraft a month later. Other notable operators were Iberia, SAS and Japan Air System. The last of the line was the MD88, which combined the newest power plant and an increased use of composite materials with an EFIS cockpit and advanced systems, alongside a redesigned cabin. This aircraft's maiden flight was on 15 August, 1987 and it entered service with its main user Delta on 5 January, 1988.

STATS	81/82/83/88	87
Length	45.06m (147ft 10in)	39.75m (130ft 5in)
Height	9.04m (29ft 8in)	9.30m (30ft 6in)
Wingspan	32.87m (107ft 10in)	32.87m (107ft 10in)
Typical/Max seats	144/172	117/130
Number built	1116	75

Airbus A330neo

FIRST FACTS	-900	-800
Launched	14/07/14	14/07/14
First Flight	19/10/17	06/11/18
Certification	26/09/18	N/A
First Delivery	26/11/18 TAP Portugal	N/A

Following the success of re-engining the A320, Airbus looked towards its longer-range aircraft and realised that a re-engined A330 would provide a number of efficiency savings, whilst basing it on an existing design would keep acquisition costs low. Launched at the Farnborough Airshow in 2014, the aircraft is designed to bring fuel burn savings of 25 per cent, as well as an increase in range of 400nm over the A330-300. The aircraft is powered by the RR Trent 700 engine and sports a new wing with composite sharklets (winglets in Airbus speak). In addition, Airbus have added what they term their 'Airspace' cabin, which not only looks better but also provides more personal space, has their latest in-flight entertainment and a quieter cabin.

The first neo – the A330-900 – took to the skies for the first time on 19 October, 2017 and received its certification on 26 September, 2018, with the first delivered to launch customer TAP on 26 November, 2018. The -900 fuselage length is the same as the -300 but with what is termed cabin optimisation, which will mean it can hold an extra 10 passengers, totalling 310, plus an extra six in the -800, which is based on the -200. Air Asia X, a major factor in the decision to re-engine the A330, have 66 on order, with Delta, Garuda and Iran Air all having made large orders, although the latter is now in doubt due to the re-introduction of sanctions by the US. All but eight of the total 242 orders are for the -900. This leaves the -800, which made its first flight on 6 November, 2018, in a precarious position having just one order for eight aircraft from Kuwait Airways, gained a few months after the loss of the original launch customer Hawaiian and its order for two aircraft.

STATS	-900	-800
Length	63.66m (208ft 9in)	58.82m (193ft)
Height	16.79m (55ft 1in)	17.39m (57ft 1in)
Wingspan	64.00m (210ft)	64.00m (210ft)
Typical/Max seats	287/440	257/406
Number ordered (02/19)	270	8

Yakovlev YAK40

Designed to replace increasingly obsolete turboprop aircraft such as the IL12 and Lisunov Li2, the Yak 40 is a 24-32 seat, pressurised trijet and possibly the world's first successful small capacity regional jet. It was the first Soviet-built airliner to be designed to western airworthiness standards. The first flight took place on 21 October, 1966, and certification followed in 1968, with Aeroflot – the type's major user – putting the aircraft into service on 30 September, 1968. As with all Soviet types, there were a myriad of variants from minor modifications to increase range to military uses including Elint intelligence gathering. Over 1,000 of these aircraft were produced and some still remain in service today, mainly in VIP configuration.

FIRST FACTS

First Flight	21/10/66
Certification	1968
Entered service	30/09/68 Aeroflot

STATS

Length	20.36m (66ft 10in)
Height	6.50m (21ft 4in)
Wingspan	25.00m (82ft)
Typical/Max seats	24/32
Number built	1,000+

Bombardier/Canadair CL215/415

FIRST FACTS	CL215	CL415
Launched	02/66	1993
First Flight	23/10/67	06/12/93
First Delivery	06/69 Sécurité Civile	11/94

The CL215 is a twin-engined, high-winged, piston-powered amphibious aircraft specifically designed for the firefighting role. It came about when Canadian government departments were looking for a better way to fight forest fires, which caused considerable destruction every year. The design was originally to be an amphibious transport aircraft until this idea was shelved in favour of the firefighting design.

This design was given the go ahead in early 1966, with the maiden flight taking place on 23 October, 1967, but the first delivery wasn't made to a Canadian operator, instead going to the French organisation the Sécurité Civile in June 1969. It went on to serve government firefighting agencies in Greece, Italy, Spain, Thailand, Venezuela, Yugoslavia (as was) as well as eight Canadian provinces.

Based on the success of the 215, Canadair went on to produce the CL415, which has an updated cockpit, increased speed and operating weight as well as a much-improved firefighting capability including the use of foam. The aircraft can scoop water from any source that has at least 1,340m (4,400ft) of flyable area. The aircraft takes just 12 seconds to scoop up over 6,000 litres of water during a 410m (1,350ft) run on it.

STATS	CL215	CL415
Length	19.82m (65ft)	19.82m (65ft)
Height	8.92m (29ft 3in)	8.92m (29ft 3in)
Wingspan	28.60m (93ft 10in)	28.60m (93ft 10in)
Number built	125	90

Airbus A340

FIRST FACTS	-200	-300	-500	-600
Launched	05/06/87	05/06/87	1997	1997
First Flight	25/10/91	01/04/92	11/02/02	23/04/01
Certification	22/12/92	22/12/92	03/12/02	N/A
First Delivery	02/02/93 Lufthansa	26/02/93 Air France	11/03 Emirates	07/02 Virgin Atlantic
Entered service	15/03/93 Lufthansa	N/A Air France	11/03 Emirates	N/A Virgin Atlantic

Airbus launched the A340 in tandem with the A330, with the 340 being the long-haul, four-engined model. The initial and ultimately the most successful version, being nearly two thirds of all 340s produced, was the A340-300. The aircraft's maiden flight took place on 25 October, 1991, with the -200 flying just a short while later on 1 April, 1992. The A340 shares much of its design and construction with the twin-engined A330 – fuselage lengths, flight deck commonality and basic airframe being just a few examples, but the biggest difference of course was that it had four engines rather than two. One benefit of having four engines was that twin-engine ETOPS did not exist at the time it was designed,

which meant this aircraft was free to fly wherever its operators wished to go.

Following certification on 22 December, 1992, the first aircraft to be delivered was a -200 on 2 February, 1993 to Lufthansa, the first -300 going to Air France a few days later on the 26th. This aircraft was the 1,000th Airbus to be delivered.

In 1997 Airbus announced it was going to produce two new variants. The first of these was the -600, aimed at replacing early model 747s. At one time the longest commercial airliner in the world, having been stretched by 12m (39ft 4in) more than the -300, it made its first flight on 23 April, 2001, with Virgin Atlantic placing it into service in August the following year.

The final version, the -500, first flew on 11 February, 2002 and became, at the time, the world's longest range commercial airliner. It was stretched 4.3m (14ft 1in) over the -300. Having the ability to fly 9,000 nautical miles meant it was capable of flying the longest non-stop commercial route in the world, SIA's New York - Singapore. This range was increased even further when, on 13 October, 2006, the -500IGW (Increased Gross Weight) model took to the skies offering a range of 9,200nm.

Numbers of these graceful aircraft are quickly reducing, and of the total 377 built there were just 159 (as at July 2018) remaining in service, mainly in Europe with Lufthansa and Iberia.

STATS	-200	-300	-500	-600
Length	59.40m (195ft)	63.70m (208ft 11in)	67.93m (222ft 10in)	75.36m (247ft 3in
Height	16.80m (55ft 3in)	16.99m (55ft 9in)	17.53m (56ft 8in)	17.93m (58ft 10in)
Wingspan	60.30m (197ft 10in)	60.30m (197ft 10in)	63.45m (208ft 2in)	63.45m (208ft 2in)
Typical/Max seats	261/303	277/440	293/440	326/475
No. built	28	218	34	97

Embraer 110 Bandeirante

ROY CARTLEDGE

Possibly the foundation stone for the Embraer we see today, the Bandeirante was initially designed for both civil and military use, and it was in its military guise, the YC-95, that it made its maiden flight on 26 October, 1968. The aircraft opened up areas of Brazil to regional air transport that previously had none and also found considerable success in the export market doing just the same. Embraer as a company was not actually formed until about a year later and took over the production of the 18-seat twin turboprop airliner. The first production Bandeirante, now with the designation EMB 110, was slightly longer than the prototypes and first flew on 9 August, 1972, with deliveries commencing to the Brazilian Air Force the following February. The first civilian customer was Trans Brasil, and they received their first aircraft in March 1973. The aircraft was also used in a variety of roles including Aerial survey, Search and Rescue, Radio calibration, and Maritime patrol. 501 of this versatile aircraft were built and some even remain in service today with operators including Air Raratonga, Islena Airlines and the Brasilian Federal Police.

FIRST FACTS

First Flight	26/10/68
Certification	1972
First delivery	09/02//3 Brasilian Air Force

STATS

Length	15.10m (49ft 6in)
Height	4.92m (16ft 2in)
Wingspan	15.33m (50ft 3in)
Typical/Max seats	18/19
Number built	501

Airbus A300

FIRST FACTS

	First Flight	First Order	Airline	First delivery	Airline
A300B1	28/10/72	N/A	N/A	11/74	TEA
B2	15/04/74	00/09/70	Air France (LOI)	10/05/74	Air France
B3	28/06/73	N/A	N/A	N/A	N/A
B4	27/12/74	09/74	Korean A/L	23/05/75	Germanair
600	08/07/83	N/A	N/A	03/84	Saudia
600R	09/12/87	N/A	American	21/04/88	American
600F	12/93	N/A	Federal Express	04/94	Federal Express
600ST	09/94	N/A	N/A	01/96	Airbus

The origins of the A300 can be traced back to July 1967 when French, British and German Ministers agreed, 'for the purpose of strengthening European co-operation in the field of aviation technology and thereby promoting economic and technological progress in Europe, to take appropriate measures for the joint development and production of an airbus.'

The official birth of the A300 came nearly two years later on 29 May,1969 at that year's Paris Airshow, when ministers from France and Germany signed an agreement officially launching the A300, which was to be the first twin-engined, widebody passenger jet in the world. This was in fact the formal launch of the company Airbus.

European governments entered into this agreement in an attempt to ward off an ever-increasing dominance from across the Atlantic. Previous European companies had produced some of the best passenger aircraft; however, the economic truth was that without joint working and co-operation in development and production these companies or indeed their individual governments could no longer compete with the US giants.

Although having had a taste of co-operation with the Anglo-French Concorde, Europe needed something with more prospects and with the growing demand for air travel a short/medium haul aircraft had much greater chances of success.

The birth of the A300 was, by default, the birth of Airbus and as such it had to be decided just how and where the aircraft should be constructed. Roger Beteille, the technical director of the A300 programme, drew up the workshare plan which has changed very little over the years. Major components were to be made by the main partners. The cockpit, control systems and the lower centre section of fuselage were to be made in France, the wings by Hawker Siddeley in the UK with the Germans making the forward and rear fuselage as well as the upper centre section. The Dutch would make the moving parts of the wing such as flaps and spoilers, with the Spanish building the horizontal tailplane. This geographic split was made to use all the available talents and capacities regardless of country.

The aircraft was designed with just two engines, which at the time was a bold move. The direct competition of the A300 was the US-built DC10 and L1011 Tristar, both with three engines. Considered the norm for the routes/distances expected from such an aircraft, this required an engine that simply did not exist. Rolls Royce promised a version of the RB211, the RB207. However, this engine never made it beyond initial development. Airbus were making a plane that had no engines!

A near disaster very quickly became a benefit. The original plan for the aircraft was for it to seat 300, hence the name. However, with major European airlines revising passenger growth forecasts it soon became clear that 250 seats over a 1,200 nautical mile range might be more suited, and with this reduction in size came the ability to purchase current engines and therefore not incur ex-

pensive development costs. Three different manufacturers had suitable engines, thereby making the aircraft a lot more attractive to prospective customers. A team working in secret came up with a new design based on these figures and this, the A300B, was the version launched at the Paris Airshow in 1969.

A key to the success of the programme was to make the aircraft as economical to operate as possible. The aircraft was designed with enough space in the hold to fit standard LD3 freight containers side by side, so increasing the profitability of each flight by carrying more cargo.

Hawker Siddeley, who despite the pull out of the UK government had continued as a sub-contractor, designed a new wing that provided greater lift, improving the A300's performance. Airbus also claimed that the aircraft would reach cruising altitude quicker than its competitors, giving the crew more time for the in-flight service.

With the aircraft being fabricated all around Europe, there was another challenge to be overcome: just how to get everything together to assemble the aircraft? The final assembly was to be in Toulouse, south western France and 160km (99 miles) from the sea. The prototype sections were all moved by sea and road but this was a far from ideal scenario. Ironically, the company looked to the US for the answer which came in the form of the US-built Super Guppy, which was a development of the military version of the Boeing Stratocruiser. This aircraft flew major components directly from the construction sites to Toulouse.

Having initially reduced the size of the aircraft, Airbus learnt that an all-economy, 250-seat aircraft was too small for a major target airline – Air France. So, the design team created 20 more seats with a small fuselage stretch, thereby creating the A300B2 (the B1 being the original 250 seater) which directly led to the programme's first order as Air France signed a letter of intent for six B2s on 3 September, 1970.

Saturday, 28 October, 1972 saw the aircraft's first flight, a month ahead of schedule. The flight lasted one hour 23 minutes, with Aerospatiale veteran Max Fischl at the controls and Bernard Ziegler the Head of Flight test as number two which reversed a tradition of 'the boss' being in charge of such an event.

Airbus knew that if the aircraft and indeed the company were to succeed they would have to make inroads into the lucrative US market, so in September 1973 the aircraft undertook a six-week tour of the Americas with everything needed on board the aircraft, from engineers to spares as well as crates of Champagne for the many VIPs expected to view it.

Air France also had the honour of performing the first commercial flight of the aircraft from Paris to London Heathrow on 23 May, 1974.

In September 1974, after discussions over a longer-range version, the B4 was designed. Korean Airlines ordered four of the long-range model plus two options, becoming the first non-European airline customer. Orders from Air India, South African Airways and Air Inter followed soon after, but the big breakthrough came with the first orders from the USA. A brave decision was taken to lease four aircraft to Eastern for six months with the promise that if they decided not to buy, then the aircraft could simply be returned to Airbus.

The gamble worked and Frank Borman of Eastern ordered 23 A300B4s with a further nine options in March 1978.

An upgraded and enhanced A300 – the A300-600 – first flew on 8 July, 1983. The new version incorporated an electronic cockpit which introduced the innovative forward facing crew cockpit, only requiring two crew members, improved wing design and a longer fuselage that could carry up to 361 passengers in a single class configuration. Another first came in 1977 when the A300B4 became the first ETOPS-compliant aircraft

The A300 has been given some interesting uses including a Zero G - reduced gravity – aircraft; however, the most innovative use of the A300 was by Airbus themselves. A larger alternative to the Super Guppy was needed and in September 1994 the A300-600ST or Beluga flew for the first time, entering service 16 months later transporting component parts for the ever-growing family of Airbus aircraft between its European sites.

The very first A300 to enter service was an Air France B2 version on 23 May, 1974

There were a total of 567 A300s delivered, of which 229 remain in service as of April 2017.

Antonov AN24/26

FIRST FACTS	AN24	AN26
Launched	1957	03/68
First Flight	29/10/59	21/05/69
First Delivery	09/62 Aeroflot	1970 Soviet Air Force

Designed, as most Soviet-era airliners were, to meet an Aeroflot requirement and to operate from short unpaved strips, it was intended to replace the IL14 on regional services with 32-40 seats. Given the NATO codename of 'Coke', the AN24 first flew on 29 October, 1959, and after a period of route proving by Aeroflot it entered service with them in 1963. Quite early on in its life the aircraft was upgraded, getting more powerful engines and seating for up to 50. Variants of the aircraft have included the AN24RV, which had an auxiliary turbojet, and the AN24P for dropping firefighters into forest fire areas. Two freight versions, the AN24T and AN24RT, have been created providing a central cargo door. The RT has been further developed into

the AN26, which has a rear loading ramp as well as yet more powerful engines. Given the NATO codenamed 'Curl', it made its first flight on 21 May, 1969 with the Soviet Air Force putting it into service in the early 1970s.

As is the norm with Soviet designs, there are a considerable number of variants from ambulance to firefighting and research to electronic warfare in addition to its 'standard' civilian roles. Other operators of the AN24 are closely connected with former soviet states and include Balkan Bulgarian, Cubana, Interflug, Tarom and LOT. China's Xian Aircraft Company has been building a version of the AN24 as the Y7 since 1970, which has brought the total number produced to 1,367 with slightly more than that at 1,403 of the AN26.

STATS	AN24	AN26
Length	23.53m (77ft 2in)	23.80m (78ft 1in)
Height	8.32m (27ft 3in)	8.57m (28ft 2in)
Wingspan	29.20m (95ft 10in)	29.20m (95ft 10in)
Typical/Max seats	44/52	40/40
No. ordered	1,367	1,403

NOVEMBER

Airbus A330ceo

FIRST FACTS	-200	-200F	-300	B/XL
First Flight	13/08/97	05/11/09	02/11/92	19/07/18
Certification	12/97	03/10	21/10/93	N/A
First Delivery	1993 Air Inter	07/10 Etihad Cargo	N/A ILFC	N/A N/A
Entered service	17/01/94 Air Inter	Etihad Cargo	Canada 3000	

The A330 is nearly identical to its four-engined stablemate the A340, apart from the obvious two engines rather than four. Launched alongside the A340 in 1987, its systems are nearly identical. However, this medium to long-range airliner didn't make its first flight until more than a year after the A340, the first variant being the larger -300. This maiden flight took place on 2 November, 1992 and later became the first aircraft to achieve simultaneous JAA and FAA certification. Launch customer Air Inter took delivery of the first aircraft in January 1994. The next and shorter version didn't take to the skies until five years later on 13 August, 1997. The customer list is extensive, major users including Lufthansa, Turkish Airlines, Delta and a number of Chinese operators. Both of these versions enabled Airbus to tap into the ever-emerging market for long-range twins.

Airbus announced that A340 production had ceased on 10 November, 2011; however, the A330 is still in production today and with the two new neo versions it is set to be for some time to come.

Airbus also produced an all-freight version based on the -200, which had some modifications to the nose gear, enabling the aircraft to have a level deck for loading. There is also a military version, the MRTT (Multi Role Tanker Transport), which has been sold to a number of air forces. The most interesting and iconic version is the updated Beluga transport, the A330-700 Beluga XL, which is a larger version of the standard Beluga used for transporting Airbus sections between the manufacturing and assembly stations around Europe. This first flew on 19 July, 2018.

STATS	-200	-200F	-300	B/XL
Length	59.40m (195ft)	63.70m (208ft 11in)	67.93m (222ft 10in)	63.10m (207ft)
Height	16.80m (55ft 3in)	16.99m (55ft 9in)	17.53m (56ft 8in)	18.90m (62ft)
Wingspan	60.30m (197ft 10in)	60.30m (197ft 10in)	63.45m (208ft 2in)	60.30m (197ft 10in)
Typical/Max seats	256/293	N/A	295/440	N/A
No. ordered (02/19)	665	42	789	5

Bombardier/Canadair CL600 Challenger

The first in a long line of highly successful business jets and the basis of the equally long line of regional jets was not actually first envisaged by Canadair but by Bill Lear. However, not having the capabilities to move forward with the design, Canadair took it on and over time evolved the design until mid-1976 when it was frozen and work started on testing and construction.

By the time of the first flight on 8 November, 1978 the aircraft had well over 100 orders despite its launch customer FedEx changing their mind and cancelling their order for 25. Certification was achieved in 1980 despite a crash during flight testing which took the life of one of the flight crew. The aircraft has gone on to operate with many commercial and military/government operators and it is still in production today as the Global Express, with total sales now well into four figures.

FIRST FACTS

First Flight	08/11/78
Certification	11/08/80

STATS

Length	20.85m (68ft 5in)
Height	6.30m (20ft 8in)
Wingspan	19.61m (64ft 4in)
Typical/Max seats	9/19
Number built	1,100+

Bombardier/Canadair CL44

FIRST FACTS	CL44	CL44D-4
First Flight	15/11/59	16/11/60
First Delivery	07/60	07/61
	RCAF	Seaboard World

In the early 1950s Canadair had acquired the rights to licence build the Bristol Britannia. One of two separate designs was the CL44, which was a re-engined version with a stretched and pressurised fuselage. This initial version was named the Yukon and all 12 produced were operated by the RCAF, including the prototype which made its maiden flight on 15 November, 1959.

Following on from this, Canadair produced a version for commercial use. It had a hinged rear fuselage for easy loading capabilities. This version, the CL44D-4, first flew on 16 November, 1960 and went into service with Flying Tiger, Slick and Seaboard World. All 27 airframes were mainly freighters; however, Loftleider used this and the

following stretched version – the CL44J – as passenger aircraft on transatlantic routes. One aircraft was modified by Conroy, who gave it a greatly increased upper fuselage for use as a high-volume freight aircraft. Many CL44s of all variants found second homes, all as freighters, with airlines like Cargolux, Transmeridien Air Cargo and Heavilift.

STATS	CL44	CL44D-4
Length	41.73m (136ft 11in)	41.73m (136ft 11in)
Height	11.16m (36ft 8in)	11.16m (36ft 8in)
Wingspan	43.37m (142ft 3in)	43.37m (142ft 3in)
Typical seats	178	178

Lockheed L1011 Tristar

FIRST FACTS	L1011-1	L1011-500
First Flight	16/11/70	16/10/78
First Delivery	05/04/72	27/04/79
	Eastern	British Airways

The Tristar came about from the same requirements specified by American Airlines that resulted in the DC10, so the similarities in overall design are not that surprising. The aircraft was the first entry into the commercial airliner market for Lockheed since it produced the L188 Electra, and the company was keen to re-enter this market, a decision some might say, in hindsight, was not the most sensible.

Lockheed went for a high-technology and subsequently high-priced design in stark contrast to Douglas and the DC10. This and the commitment to Rolls Royce created a beautiful looking, technologically advanced and quiet airliner. However, Rolls Royce were having their own difficulties and went into receivership, thus halting the final assembly, and with no other real engine option the future looked bleak. Fortunately, the UK government bailed out Rolls Royce, ensuring a future for the engine with the L1011. However, the Tristar was always behind the DC10 in giving the mar-

ket what it needed and never matched their rival's success. The prototype first flew on 16 November, 1970, achieving certification on 14 April, 1972 with first deliveries being made to launch customer Eastern Airlines soon after. It had an advanced autopilot system which enabled it to become the first wide-bodied aircraft to achieve FAA certification for CAT-IIIC auto landing. The aircraft went on to sell 250 to some famous names in aviation

such as TWA, Pan Am, Air Canada, British Airways and Cathay Pacific, who operated the biggest fleet outside the USA, with the honour of the largest fleet going to Delta. Although there were a number of versions created to increase and improve performance, the only substantially different version was the L-1011-500, which at 4.30m (14ft) shorter than the original was a longer-range model with more powerful RR engines and a greater wingspan. Flying for the first time on 16 October,

1978, it became popular with operators on international routes, including British Airways who operated a number of the type and introduced the first services after taking delivery on 27 April, 1979. The aircraft went on to find homes with a variety of mainly charter operators once its original owners replaced them with newer, more efficient aircraft, as well as with the RAF as tanker transport aircraft, although it is thought that none remain in service today.

STATS	L1011-1	L1011-500
Length	54.17m (177ft 8in)	50.05m (164ft 2in)
Height	16.87m (55ft 4in)	16.87m (55ft 4in)
Wingspan	47.35m (155ft 4in)	50.09m (164ft 4in)
Typical/Max seats	256/400	246/330
Number Built	160 of 249	50 of 249

Fokker F27

FIRST FACTS	100/200/300/400	500
First Flight	24/11/55	15/11/67
First Delivery	11/58	05/68
	Aer Lingus	KLM

One of the most successful aircraft of its time, the F27 was designed as yet another potential DC3 replacement; in fact, Fokker spoke with a number of DC3 operators about what they might want from any replacement. Initially aimed at being a 32-seat model, by the time of its first flight on 24 November, 1955 it had become capable of carrying 36 passengers and had received the name 'Friendship'. It took a further three years before it entered revenue service with Aer Lingus in December 1958. Momentum for the aircraft was slow to build, but in 1960 Fokker received a number of orders as the types reputation increased. Early users of the type were Braathens, SAFE, TAA, Ansett and Luxair. There were a number of

versions based on the original model which provided more powerful engines and the ability to carry cargo. Fairchild in the USA also licence built a number of these early versions as well as producing a stretched version named the FH227.

The first change in the overall dimensions of the Fokker models came on 15 November, 1967 when the srs 500 first took to the skies. This model was 1.5m (4ft 11in) longer than the earlier models, enabling it to carry up to eight more passengers with initial deliveries going to home country flag carrier KLM. Overall this is possibly the best of the DC3 replacements, having outsold the competition by quite a hefty number, selling 786 including the licence-built models in the US.

STATS	100/200/300/400	500
Length	23.56m (77ft 3in)	25.06m (82ft 2in)
Height	8.51m (27ft 11in)	8.51m (27ft 11in)
Wingspan	29.00m (95ft 2in)	29.00m (95ft 2in)
Typical/Max seats	40/52	52/60
Number Built	85/138/13/218	112

Fokker 70/100

FIRST FACTS	70	100
First Flight	04/04/93	30/11/86
First Delivery	10/94	29/02/88
	Ford Motor Co	Swissair

Fokker announced this derivative of its F28 simultaneously with the F50. Based on the F28-4000, the F100 has a longer fuselage, larger redesigned wings, a new CRT flight deck and cabin redesign and it was powered by new generation Rolls Royce Tay turbofans. The prototype of this new medium-range twin turbofan regional airliner took to the skies on 30 November, 1986 with certification achieved almost exactly a year later. Swissair, the launch customer, took the first airframe on 29 February, 1988. TAM, KLM, US Air and American Airlines also took considerable numbers into their fleets. In a sign of things to come, the aircraft was of multinational construction as it was produced in collaboration with Deutsche Airbus, who produced large fuselage sections and the tail section, and Shorts, who manufactured the wings.

Both longer and shorter versions of the aircraft were considered, but it was just the shorter Fokker 70 that was produced. In typical configuration, the aircraft would hold 79 passengers as opposed to the F100s 97. The first of this version to fly was in fact a modified F100, and it did so on 4 April, 1993. Compared to the 100, the 70 was 4.62m (15ft 3in) shorter and the first delivery was made to the Ford Motor Company in October 1994, with Korean Airlines being the first airline two months later. Both versions sold well, particularly the 100, but came at a time when Fokker and its partners were having considerable financial difficulties and the company eventually failed after just over 330 had been delivered. Although being phased out, there are some pockets of resistance around the world, with Australasia being quite an area of use, from homegrown Alliance Airlines and Virgin Australia to Air Niugini still using them. Considered a good choice for certain tasks in certain areas of the world, Fokker are still marketing the aircraft but only for pre-used examples.

STATS	70	100
Length	30.91m (101ft 5in)	35.53m (116ft 7in)
Height	8.51m (27ft 11in)	8.51m (27ft 11in)
Wingspan	28.08m (92ft 2in)	28.08m (92ft 2in)
Typical/Max seats	72/85	97/122
Number Built	48	283

DECEMBER

Bristol 170 Freighter

FIRST FACTS	MKI/II/XI/21/31	MK32
First Flight	02/12/45	16/01/53

Another aircraft to emerge from the Brabazon Committee's findings in 1944, the Bristol 170 was designed as a utilitarian, rugged and low-cost aircraft aimed at a variety of roles, both passenger and freight in both commercial and military operations. The prototype made its first flight on 2 December, 1945. Two main versions were produced, although throughout its production it was modified to provide greater weights as well as having more powerful engines fitted. One of them was for all-passenger use and named the Wayfarer and the other was possibly the more well-known version, which had clam shell doors under the cockpit allowing freight to be loaded straight in and thereby making full use of the available space. This model found a niche with cross-channel ferry companies as passenger vehicles could simply be driven into the aircraft. The final version – the Mk32 – was a stretched version for Silver City Airways who wanted to carry more cars on their services. It made its first flight on 16 January, 1953. The aircraft found use with a considerable number of operators, including Channel Air Bridge, Air Vietnam, Hunting Air Surveys, Dan Air, Wardair and SAFE. It also worked for the military in countries like Burma, Canada, Australia and New Zealand, selling 214 of all variants.

STATS		
Length	20.83m (68ft 4in)	22.35m (73ft 4in)
Height	6.60m (21ft 8in)	6.60m (21ft 8in)
Wingspan	32.92m (108ft)	32.92m (108ft)
Typical/Max seats	2 cars+15/32	3 cars+23/60

Dornier 328

Looking to grow the successful 228, Dornier initially started the process of designing a 30-seat airliner in 1986, but the project was soon halted while the company looked into just what the market at the time needed. Following resumption of the project in August 1988, three development aircraft were produced with the first prototype taking to the skies above Oberpfaffenhofen on 6 December, 1991, by which time a number of orders had been placed including a significant order of 35 from US feeder Horizon Air. Immediately following JAA certification, the first aircraft was delivered to Air Engiadina on 13 October, 1993 with Horizon's arriving the following month following FAA certification.

The aircraft was headed for difficult times, however, with a recession looming and the subsequent failure of the Dornier Fairchild company, as well as its successor AvCraft Aviation. Additionally facing increasing competition from not only similar turboprops but early generation regional jets, manufacture of the aircraft eventually ceased in 2000 after production of 217 units were delivered to customers including Loganair, Air Alps, Air Wisconsin and Sun Air.

A jet-powered version was later produced, making its first flight on 20 January, 1998 (see separate entry).

FIRST FACTS

First Flight	06/12/91
Certification	10/93
First Delivery	13/10/93 Air Engiadina

STATS

Length	21.22m (69ft 8in)
Height	7.20m (23ft 8in)
Wingspan	20.98m (68ft 10in)
Typical/Max seats	30/33
Number built	217

Lockheed L188 Electra

This aircraft was initially developed to meet a need expressed by American Airlines for a four-engined, short to medium-range airliner capable of carrying 75-100 passengers. The program had an excellent start with nearly 150 orders from both within the US and from Europe and the Pacific prior to its maiden flight on 6 December, 1957. This level of positivity did not, however, continue. Initial deliveries were made to American Airlines but with their pilots on strike the aircraft's service entry had to wait until 1959 when Eastern received their first examples. Worse was to come as by 1960 there had been three separate and fatal crashes involving the aircraft breaking up in flight, which was eventually found to be due to an engine-mounting defect.

Lockheed redesigned the aircraft and it served reliably with many airlines including Varig who used it on their famous Ponte Aérea Rio de Janeiro - São Paulo shuttle service, but the damage had already been done. Add to that the dawn of the jet age and, like the Bristol Britannia, the aircraft was fast becoming outmoded. 55 of the new L188C version were built amounting to a total of just 170 overall.

The story doesn't quite end there, however; many aircraft went on to find new uses, mainly as freighters, and some remain in service today with Buffalo Airways in Canada's northern territories, a major user, as well as other organisations using it as an aerial firefighting platform.

The airframe, despite the early crashes, was a sound one and it went on to form the basis of the P3 Orion, which is still active today and sold many times more than its ancestor.

FIRST FACTS	
First Flight	06/12/57
Certification	10/93
First Delivery	12/58 American Airlines
Entered service	01/59 Eastern

STATS	
Length	31.85m (104ft 6in)
Height	10.00m (32ft 10in)
Wingspan	30.18m (99ft)
Typical/Max seats	65/98
Number built	170 (115 L188A 55 L188C)

Boeing 787 Dreamliner

FIRST FACTS	-8	-9	-10
First Flight	15/12/09	17/09/13	31/03/17
Certification	26/08/11	05/06/14	01/18
First Delivery	25/09/11	09/07/14	25/03/18
	ANA	Air New Zealand	Singapore Airlines

The first in a new breed of super-efficient, twin-engined airliners, the 787 Dreamliner was the first to have its airframe constructed primarily from composite materials. Studies into the design go as far back as 2001, although it wasn't until 2004 that the product was formally launched. Boeing decided that it would build the aircraft in a different way to previously by joining up completed sub-assemblies at its Everett factory and later at the new assembly line at Charlotte North Carolina rather than build the aircraft from scratch. It is a truly multinational effort with subcontractors being from all parts of the globe. This new method of construction required large sub-assemblies being transported to the assembly factories and Boeing modified four used 747-400s into outsize cargo aircraft named 'Dreamlifters'. The first flight was originally intended for August 2007 but a variety of delays impacted on this significantly enough

for some airlines to start talking about compensation. Further issues with the aircraft were reportedly it was overweight and therefore unable to meet predicted range forecasts, which did not help matters. The first Dreamliner, a -8, finally took to the skies for the first time on 15 December, 2009 from Paine Field.

The programme's difficulties continued into flight testing, from problems with the Rolls Royce Trent 1000 to an in-flight fire causing an emergency landing. However, certification was eventually granted (although having taken twice as long as expected), which paved the way for the first aircraft to be delivered to All Nippon Airlines (ANA) on 25 September, 2011. Initial passenger reports were very favourable, particularly about the cabin environment.

The larger -9 model has two 10ft plugs forward and aft of the wing, with revisions to the wing and systems. The aircraft's maiden flight was on 17 September, 2013 with first delivery to Air New Zealand on 9 July, 2014. The latest version to take to the skies is the -10, which is the only 787 to be assembled exclusively at Charleston. First flight from there took place on 31 March, 2017, with Singapore Airlines this time taking the first aircraft on 23 March, 2018.

Problems have continued to dog the programme throughout its development. Fuel leaks on a number of aircraft caused a number of concerns both with the FAA in the US and in Japan as a number of the leaks had been found on ANA aircraft. A further, well documented, issue surrounded the use of lithium metal batteries causing an eventual grounding of the aircraft for a period of time. Although the visual problem was mainly confined to smoke and heat damage, on 12 July, 2013 a fire to a fortunately empty Ethiopian Airlines aircraft caused considerable

damage. More current issues surround the Rolls Royce Trent engine which, after numerous in-flight shutdowns, has required the grounding again of certain aircraft until the identified issues have been fixed.

Despite all these issues, the aircraft has sold nearly 1,400 of all versions, with about half of these already delivered, and it is saving the world's airlines money with the overall efficiencies it brings.

STATS	-8	-9	-10
Length	56.72m (186ft 1in)	62.81m (206ft 1in)	68.28m (224ft)
Height	17.09m (56ft 1in)	17.09m (56ft 1in)	17.09m (56ft 1in)
Wingspan	60.12m (197ft 3in)	60.12m (197ft 3in)	60.12m (197ft 3in)
Typical/Max seats	242/359	290/406	330/440
Total ordered (01/19)	444	804	173

Antonov AN12

Although primarily a military design, about 30 per cent of the AN12 production run was delivered to commercial freight operators. Initial operators included LOT, Iraqi Airways and Egyptair. However, not surprisingly it was Aeroflot who took the first civilian model after the type's first flight on 16 December, 1957. It went on to sell over 1,200 of all the various models produced as well as the licence-built models in China under the name of Shaanxi Y-8. A number are still in service today, hauling freight, mainly with operators from the ex-Soviet republics.

FIRST FACTS

First Flight	16/12/57
First Delivery	1958 Soviet Air Force

STATS

Length	33.10m (108ft 7in)
Height	9.83m (32ft 3in)
Wingspan	38.00m (124ft 8in)
Number built	1,248

Douglas DC3

First Flight	17/12/35
Entered service	25/06/36
	American Airlines

The term legend is grossly overused in today's society; however, not in regard to the venerable DC3 Dakota. It is quite possibly the single most important transport aircraft ever to exist, and at over 10,000 built probably the most widely used aircraft as well. Despite making its first flight back on 17 December, 1935, there are still examples flying today, even in scheduled airline service with Buffalo Airways in Canada.

The aircraft came about because of a difficulty in TWA acquiring the new, all-metal Boeing 247, with Boeing-owned United having the first 60 off the production line. Not being in a position to wait for the aircraft, TWA approached manufacturers with a set of criteria for its own twin-engined, all-metal airliner with the ability to operate from what we would now call 'hot and high' airfields on just one engine. This initially led to the DC1, which made its first flight on 1 July, 1933. By the time the aircraft

was ordered by TWA, it had received a number of refinements and a new designation, the DC2.

Another US airline, this time American Airlines, also played a major role in the development of the DC3 as they asked Douglas for a larger DC2 to replace the Curtiss T-32 on transcontinental sleeper services, and on 17 December, 1935 a true legend was born when the DC3 first took to the skies on its maiden flight. Produced initially in two versions, one being exactly what American had asked for, the 14-seat DST, the Douglas Sleeper Transport, and the more standard 21-seat airliner, it quickly gained an excellent reputation with both commercial and military operators following its entry into service with American on 25 June, 1936. Many of the large US carriers at the time operated the aircraft, including TWA, Delta and Eastern, in addition to launch customer American and even United, whose choice of the Boeing 247 had started off this aircraft's remarkable journey.

With the advent of war in Europe, in addition to commercial airliners being taken in to military service, the DC3 found itself being produced in huge numbers as the C-47 Skytrain and C-53 Skytrooper, as well as Lisunov LI-2 licence-built versions in the Soviet Union. It was these thousands of aircraft that found their way into the vast majority of post-war airlines once hostilities ceased in 1945. Production went back to the civilian version and the aircraft remained in airline service for many years. Douglas did try to stretch and upgrade the aircraft with more powerful engines and improved looks and performance; however, despite this Super DC3 taking to the skies in August 1949, it fell victim to its predecessor's success as there were simply too many military surplus 'standard' DC3s available so it was simply not economical to buy a new one.

Loved by flight crew and passengers alike, even when newer and larger capacity piston and jet airliners came on to the market the DC3 just kept on flying, finding homes with second-level operators all around the world, and this kept on happening – each time the current airline type made room for newer types, the DC3 kept on finding a new home and new markets to serve. The ever-present DC3 is still in service around the world today, over 80 years after its first flight, performing many roles from crop spraying to skydiving platforms to freight and sightseeing services, the latter simply because of the aircraft itself! There are also many preserved in museums and flying on the airshow circuit.

There have been a number of attempts to modify the aircraft with the addition of Turboprop engines, the most notable being Basler, who still today are modifying the DC3 with Pratt and Whitney PT6A turboprop engines to make it stage III noise compli-

ant whilst at the same time stretching the fuselage and fully refurbishing the aircraft for its future role.

A total of 16,079 of all variants are said to have been produced – 607 civil variants, 10,048 C-47s and C-53s, 4,937 LI-2s and 487 licence-built L2Ds by Mitsubishi in Japan.

Throughout this book you will have seen reference to manufacturers looking to build a DC3 replacement, some with better success than others, and this in itself is a testament to the abilities of this iconic aircraft. However, there is a common saying in aviation circles and it applies to perhaps two or three aircraft in total, but mostly to this one in particular: 'The only replacement for a DC3 is another DC3', and at 80 years young who can disagree with that?

STATS	
Length	19.70m (64ft 8in)
Height	5.16m (16ft 11in)
Wingspan	29.00m (95ft 2in)
Number built	16,079

Boeing 707

FIRST FACTS	120	220	320	320B	320C	420
First Flight	20/12/57	N/A	11/01/59	31/01/62	19/02/63	19/05/59
Entered service	26/10/58	12/59	08/59	06/62	N/A	04/60
	American A/L	Braniff	Pan Am	Pan Am	N/A	BOAC
Number Built	72	5	69	175	337	37
Typical/Max seats	110/174	121/189	121/189	121/199	121/215	121/189

Boeings first jetliner, the 707, was originally known as the dash 80 as it was developed from a prototype – the Boeing 367-80 – which first flew in 1954, and although few are still flying the aircraft lives on in many of Boeing's new aircraft as elements of their fuselages are still the same design today. The 367-80 was actually designed as a tanker transporter which, of course, the 707 went on to become later in its career. It first flew on 15 July, 1954; however, the first flight of what became the 707 didn't happen until many years later and after a number of design changes both through Boeings own design needs and those needed to compete with the DC8. The initial model designated 707-120 first took to the skies on 20 December, 1957, and with certification achieved by September the following year, launch customer Pan Am were able to get their first aircraft in service the following month, operating from New York to Paris. Although aircraft are normally stretched during their lifetime, the 707's first change was to make it shorter by 3.05m (10ft) for use by QANTAS who needed extra range. A small number of 'hot and high' aircraft were also produced for Braniff and designated the -220.

These initial variants carried up to 174 passengers and were powered by turbojets. Even though Pan Am used the aircraft on transatlantic routes, they were primarily designed for US domestic routes. That was until 11 January, 1959 when the first flight of the 707-320 Intercontinental took place. This was a stretched version of the 120 and it carried up to 189 passengers. Along with wing modifications, which included a greater fuel capacity, this aircraft was designed to live up to its name. Again, Pan Am was the launch customer, with orders also coming from Air France, TWA, Sabena and SAA. A number of aircraft fitted with early generation turbofans were delivered to Lufthansa, BOAC, El Al, Cunard and Air India with the designation 707-420, but only 37 were sold as most airlines decided to wait for the next generation on the way from Pratt and Whitney.

The change to turbofan engines as standard occurred on 31 January, 1962 with Pan Am yet again the first to put the 320B into revenue service in June of the same year. This change saw a much greater take up by the world's airlines, with 174 of the 320B being sold before the 320C eventually became the definitive version, selling 337 excluding military versions. This new standard model made its first flight on 19 February, 1963. With a number of modifications to increase range and payload, the 320C also had two additional exits which allowed a maximum of 215 passengers to be carried. Another door, this time for cargo, was also added allowing a mixture of freight and passengers to be carried. Many 707s went on to become pure freighters once the many second-ary passenger operators replaced them with more modern aircraft. The design was also used extensively by the military as tankers, transports and the impressive looking E3 Sentry, as well as being in use as the US Presidential transport.

There was one final offspring of the dash 80 and that is the 720. This was designed to be a lower-cost version than the others. The first flight was on 23 November, 1959 with launch customer United putting the aircraft into service in July 1960. Braniff, Aer Lingus and Eastern were some of the other airlines to follow suit. A turbofan version, the 720B, was also produced, making its first flight on 6 October, 1960 with American being the launch customer. Many early model 720s were converted to the 720B standard.

STATS	120/220	320/420	320B/C	720
Length	44.04m (144ft 6in)	46.61m (152ft 11in)	46.61m (152ft 11in)	41.50m (136ft 2in)
Height	12.80m (42ft)	12.80m (42ft)	12.93m (42ft 5in)	12.72m (41ft 9in)
Wingspan	39.88m (95ft 2in)	43.41 (142ft 5in)	44.42m (145ft 9in)	39.88m (130ft 10in)

Antonov AN225

FIRST FACTS

First Flight	21/12/88

A truly unique aircraft with just one in existence (although there is the majority of another still to be assembled in a building near Kiev), the AN225 Mriya is a six-engined, strategic cargo airlifter, originally conceived to transport the Soviet equivalent of the space shuttle, the Buran, as well as other parts for the Soviet space programme, and it is based on another heavylifter, the AN124. The aircraft is the heaviest ever built and sports the biggest wingspan of any aircraft in operation today. It made its maiden flight on 21 December, 1988. However, once the Buran missions finished following the collapse of the Soviet Union, so did the need for the aircraft, and it was mothballed in 1994. New life was breathed into the aircraft in the late 1990s when the organisation that was set up to make use of ex-military assets, Antonov Airlines, had decided that it needed a greater capacity than its current fleet of AN124s and 12s. The aircraft was re-engined and modified to accept heavy cargo and outsized loads and received its second certification on 23 May, 2001. Its first commercial service was on 3 January, 2002 and since then it has gone on to transport all sorts of goods including what is reported to be the

heaviest single item ever shipped by air, a generator and associated equipment, weighing in at 189 tonnes (417,000lb) and also the longest ever, a pair of wind turbine blades at 42.10m (138ft). In fact, it is said that the hold is actually longer than the world's first-ever flight by the Wright Flyer.

There have been a number of attempts to get the second aircraft completed, all of which subsequently failed, leaving the unfinished parts in a massive warehouse on the outskirts of Kiev. A headturner wherever it goes, the 225 is still in service carrying heavy and outsized loads around the world.

STATS

Length	84.00m (275ft 7in)
Height	18.10m (59ft 5in)
Wingspan	88.40m (290ft)
Number built	1

Ilyushin IL86

FIRST FACTS

First Flight	22/12/76
Entered service	26/12/80 Aeroflot

The IL86 is a four-turbofan-engined, medium-range airliner and the first Soviet-built wide body. At the 1971 Paris Airshow it was announced as a replacement for the IL62. It took five years to get the project into the air, but on 22 December, 1976 the first prototype took to the skies over Voronehz in Russia. Although initial reports were positive, with the aircraft reportedly bettering western counterparts in many ways, the design fell short in a critical factor. Not only was the design and production phase protracted, but the aircraft's Kusnetsov turbofans were thirsty, therefore making the aircraft expensive to operate and consequently difficult to make a profit.

Following on from the maiden flight, Ilyushin made over 1,400 test flights before Aeroflot took delivery, then they performed nearly 500 test flights before the first real revenue service took place on 26 December, 1980 on the Moscow – Tashkent route, with international services starting from the following summer. Aeroflot were the only airline to order from new, but following

on from the collapse of the Soviet Union the aircraft appeared in the colours of many airlines of the newly independent states in addition to some that went to China. Noise regulations brought in by the majority of the world ultimately led to the demise of the 'Camber', as NATO named it, and on 22 October, 2006 Aeroflot withdrew the aircraft from service with other operators following suit in the time that followed. Of the 106 airframes built, no civilian aircraft are thought to be in operation today, although there are some in military service.

STATS

Length	59.54m (195ft 4in)
Height	15.81m (51ft 11in)
Wingspan	48.06m (157ft 9in)
Number built	106
Typical/Max seats	234/350

Nord 262

Yet another DC3 replacement, the Nord 262 was designed as a high-wing, twin-turboprop airliner capable of seating up to 29 passengers. It made its maiden flight on 24 December, 1962 and received certification on 16 July, 1964. Operating in both civilian and military roles, 111 of them were built, used by airlines such as Japan Domestic, Templehof Airways and Dan Air in addition to launch customer Air Inter. In the US the aircraft was modified and became known as the Mohawk 298, with Allegheny Airlines the major operator. None are thought to be in service today.

FIRST FACTS	
First Flight	24/12/62
First Delivery	07/64
	Air Inter

STATS	
Length	19.28m (63ft 3in)
Height	6.21m (20ft 4in)
Wingspan	21.90m (71ft 10in)
Number built	111
Typical/Max seats	26/29

26th - 1982

Antonov AN124

The An124 Ruslan or 'Condor' in NATO speak is a long-range, heavy-lift freight aircraft. The aircraft is designed to operate completely independently from ground assistance if required. Cargo can be loaded from the front with the nose raised or from the rear ramp. Items can be self-loaded or winched on using the incorporated winches and cranes. The aircraft will even kneel down at the front to assist in the loading. The prototype first flew on 26 December, 1982, receiving civil certification on 30 December, 1992, and was at the time the largest aircraft by weight or wingspan. The major operator of the type was, and still is, the Russian Air Force; however, a civilian version – the 124-100 – was also produced, which is also still in service today. The main operators are Volga Dnepr, who also operated in conjunction with Heavylift cargo until they ceased operations in 2006, and Antonov Airlines. There are plans to upgrade and 'westernise' the aircraft for a variety of customers and time will tell if any of these ever take flight.

FIRST FACTS

First Flight	26/12/82

STATS

Length	69.10m (226ft 8in)
Height	20.78m (68ft 2in)
Wingspan	73.30m (240ft 6in)
Number built	55

Fokker 50

Development of this and its jet-powered sibling was announced on 24 November, 1983 on the 25th anniversary of its predecessor, the F27, entering airline service. Although utilising the basic wing and fuselage design of the F27, the F50 was very much a new design, having only 20 per cent commonality with the F27 with a new EFIS cockpit, digital avionics, new cabin design and the use of composite materials. The main difference, however, was a change to a more fuel efficient and quieter engine. Aimed at the same market in which the F27 sat, the prototype was actually a modified F27-500, and PH-OSO made its first flight on 28 December, 1985 with the first production model taking flight on 13 February, 1987. Certification was granted on 15 May the same year, with launch customer OLT taking the first aircraft in that August. A 'hot and high' version called the series 300 was developed, with Avianca taking the first of these in April 1993. The list of operators is considerable, stretching from the likes of SAS, VLM, Aer

Lingus and KLM in Europe through Malaysia Airlines, Philippine Airlines and Air Astana in Asia to Ansett and Flight West Airlines in Australia. Fokker stretched the aircraft by 1.62m (5ft 4in), naming it the Fokker 60. Only four were produced and all went to the Royal Netherlands Air Force. Of the 213 built, quite a number are still in service as at the end of 2018.

STATS	
Length	25.25m (82ft 10in)
Height	8.32m (27ft 4in)
Wingspan	29m (95ft 2in)
Number built	213
Typical/Max seats	50/58

Tupolev TU144

MATT FALCUS

FIRST FACTS

First Flight	31/12/68
Entered service	12/75
	Aeroflot

The story about the TU144 started off on a positive note as it became the world's first supersonic transport to fly and exceed the speed of sound (in level flight), which it did on 5 June, 1969, breaking Mach 2 on 26 May, 1970. It was also the first to enter service in December 1975. However, it was the rush to be the first in the race with Concorde that ultimately became its downfall. Corners were cut and the programme rushed, which led to a considerable number of issues and in-flight failures that became apparent quite quickly and continued into the aircraft's service.

The aircraft made its maiden flight on 31 December, 1968 from Voronezh in Russia and during the flight testing made a visit to the Paris Airshow in 1973, where the first of two crashes occurred, this one very publicly.

The aircraft initially went into service in a far from glamorous role, flying freight and mail prior to passenger services, which started the month after certification in October 1977. Unfortunately,

a further crash occurred in May the following year on a pre-delivery test flight, which, after only 55 flights, caused the grounding of passenger flights and the return to the freight role. Unfortunately, with the aircraft unable to meet necessary goals safely the project was cancelled in 1983 after just 102 scheduled flights.

Following cancellation of scheduled commercial services, some aircraft went on to become flying laboratories, including one that after extensive modification was used by NASA. Most of the aircraft are now on display at museums including one at Sinsheim in Germany where it is displayed next to Concorde, making it the only place in the world where you can see both aircraft together.

STATS

Length	65.70m (215ft 6in)
Height	12.55m (41ft)
Wingspan	28.80m (94ft 6in)
Number built	17
Typical/Max seats	140/140

ALPHABETICAL LIST OF AIRCRAFT

Alphabetical List
of Aircraft

AIRCRAFT	MY FIRST FLIGHT		
Aero Spacelines Guppy 201 24 August 1970 page 126	Date	Airline	Registration
Airbus A220-100 **(Bombardier CS100)** 16 September 2013 page 140	Date	Airline	Registration
Airbus A220-300 **(Bombardier CS300)** 27 February 2015 page 140	Date	Airline	Registration
Airbus A300-600 8 July 1983 page 157	Date	Airline	Registration
Airbus A300-600F December 1993 page 157	Date	Airline	Registration
Airbus A300-600R 9 December 1987 page 157	Date	Airline	Registration
Airbus A300-600ST 13 September 1994 page 157	Date	Airline	Registration

AIRCRAFT	MY FIRST FLIGHT		
Airbus A300B1 28 October 1972 page 157 AIRBUS	Date Airline Registration		
Airbus A300B2 15 April 1974 page 157	Date Airline Registration		
Airbus A300B4 27 December 1974 page 157	Date Airline Registration		
Airbus A310-200 3 April 1982 page 62	Date Airline Registration		
Airbus A310-300 8 July 1985 page 62	Date Airline Registration		
Airbus A318 15 January 2002 page 40	Date Airline Registration		
Airbus A319 29 August 1995 page 40	Date Airline Registration		
Airbus A319neo 31 March 2017 page 142	Date Airline Registration		

	AIRCRAFT	MY FIRST FLIGHT
	Airbus A320-100 22 February 1987 page 41	Date Airline Registration
	Airbus A320-200 page 40	Date Airline Registration
	Airbus A320neo 25 September 2014 page 142	Date Airline Registration
	Airbus A321-100 11 March 1993 page 41	Date Airline Registration
	Airbus A321-200 12 December 1996 page 41	Date Airline Registration
	Airbus A321LR 31 January 2018 page 142 HENDRIK SCHOOF	Date Airline Registration
	Airbus A321neo 9 February 2016 page 142	Date Airline Registration
	Airbus A330-200 13 August 1997 page 97	Date Airline Registration

AIRCRAFT	MY FIRST FLIGHT
Airbus A330-200F 5 November 2009 page 162	Date Airline Registration
Airbus A330-300 2 November 1992 page 162	Date Airline Registration
Airbus A330-700 Beluga XL 19 July 2018 page 162	Date Airline Registration
Airbus A330-800neo 6 November 2018 page 151 YANNIK DELAMARRE	Date Airline Registration
Airbus A330-900neo 19 October 2017 page 151	Date Airline Registration
Airbus A340-200 1 April 1992 page 154	Date Airline Registration
Airbus A340-300 25 October 1991 page 154	Date Airline Registration
Airbus A340-500 11 February 2002 page 154	Date Airline Registration

	AIRCRAFT	MY FIRST FLIGHT
	Airbus A340-500IGW 13 October 2006 page 155	Date Airline Registration
	Airbus A340-600 23 April 2001 page 154	Date Airline Registration
	Airbus A350-900 14 June 2013 page 96	Date Airline Registration
	Airbus A350-1000 24 November 2016 page 96	Date Airline Registration
	Airbus A350ULR 28 April 2018 page 97	Date Airline Registration
	Airbus A380-800 27 April 2005 page 68	Date Airline Registration
	Antonov AN2 31 August 1947 page 131	Date Airline Registration
	Antonov AN12 16 December 1957 page 175	Date Airline Registration

	AIRCRAFT	MY FIRST FLIGHT
	Antonov AN22 27 February 1965 page 47	Date Airline Registration
	Antonov AN24 29 October 1959 page 160	Date Airline Registration
	Antonov AN26 21 May 1969 page 160	Date Airline Registration
	Antonov AN72 31 August 1977 page 132	Date Airline Registration
	Antonov AN74TK-300 20 April 2001 page 132	Date Airline Registration
	Antonov AN124 26 December 1982 page 183	Date Airline Registration
	Antonov AN225 21 December 1988 page 180	Date Airline Registration
	Aviation Traders ATL.98 Carvair 21 June 1961 page 100	Date Airline Registration

LEWIS GRANT

	AIRCRAFT	MY FIRST FLIGHT
	BAC 1-11-200 20 August 1963 page 123	Date Airline Registration
	BAC 1-11-500 30 June 1967 page 123	Date Airline Registration
	BAC/Aerospatiale Concorde 2 March 1969 page 50	Date Airline Registration
	BAe 146-100 3 September 1981 page 135	Date Airline Registration
	BAe 146-200 1 August 1982 page 135	Date Airline Registration
	BAe 146-300 1 May 1987 page 135	Date Airline Registration
	BAe ATP 6 August 1986 page 116	Date Airline Registration
	BAe/Hawker Siddeley 125 13 August 1962 page 118	Date Airline Registration

	AIRCRAFT	MY FIRST FLIGHT
	BAe J31 28 March 1980 page 57	Date Airline Registration
	BAe J32 13 April 1988 page 57	Date Airline Registration
	BAe J41 25 September 1991 page 57	Date Airline Registration
	BAe RJ70 23 June 1992 page 135	Date Airline Registration
	BAe RJ85 24 March 1992 page 135	Date Airline Registration
	BAe RJ100 13 May 1992 page 135	Date Airline Registration
	Beechcraft 1900C 3 September 1982 page 137	Date Airline Registration
	Beechcraft 1900D 1 March 1990 page 137	Date Airline Registration

	AIRCRAFT	MY FIRST FLIGHT	
	Beechcraft King Air 90 20 January 1964 page 21	Date Airline Registration	
	Boeing 367-80 15 July 1954 page 178	Date Airline Registration	
	Boeing 707-120 20 December 1957 page 178	Date Airline Registration	
	Boeing 707-320 11 January 1959 page 178	Date Airline Registration	
	Boeing 707-320B 31 January 1962 page 178	Date Airline Registration	
	Boeing 707-320C 19 February 1963 page 178	Date Airline Registration	
	Boeing 707-420 19 May 1959 page 178	Date Airline Registration	
	Boeing 717-200 2 September 1998 page 134	Date Airline Registration	

	AIRCRAFT	MY FIRST FLIGHT
	Boeing 720 23 November 1959 page 179	Date Airline Registration
	Boeing 720B 6 October 1960 page 179	Date Airline Registration
	Boeing 727-100 9 February 1963 page 29	Date Airline Registration
	Boeing 727-200 27 July 1967 page 29	Date Airline Registration
	Boeing 737-100 9 April 1967 page 63 KARL MULLOCK	Date Airline Registration
	Boeing 737-200 8 August 1967 page 63	Date Airline Registration
	Boeing 737-200ADV 15 April 1971 page 64	Date Airline Registration
	Boeing 737-300 24 February 1984 page 43	Date Airline Registration

	AIRCRAFT	MY FIRST FLIGHT		
	Boeing 737-400 19 February 1988 page 43	Date Airline Registration		
	Boeing 737-500 20 June 1989 page 43	Date Airline Registration		
	Boeing 737-600 22 January 1998 page 31	Date Airline Registration		
	Boeing 737-700 9 February 1997 page 31	Date Airline Registration		
	Boeing 737-800 31 July 1997 page 31	Date Airline Registration		
	Boeing 737-900 3 August 2000 page 31	Date Airline Registration		
	Boeing 737MAX7 16 March 2018 page 24	Date Airline Registration		
	Boeing 737MAX8 29 January 2016 page 24	Date Airline Registration		

	AIRCRAFT	MY FIRST FLIGHT
	Boeing 737MAX9 13 April 2017 page 24	Date Airline Registration
	Boeing 747-8 11 March 2011 page 28	Date Airline Registration
	Boeing 747-8F 8 February 2010 page 28	Date Airline Registration
	Boeing 747-100 9 February 1969 page 33	Date Airline Registration
	Boeing 747-200B 11 October 1970 page 33	Date Airline Registration
	Boeing 747-300 5 October 1982 page 149	Date Airline Registration
	Boeing 747-400 29 April 1988 page 71	Date Airline Registration
	Boeing 747SP 4 July 1975 page 106	Date Airline Registration

	AIRCRAFT	MY FIRST FLIGHT
	Boeing 757-200 19 February 1982 page 37	Date Airline Registration
	Boeing 757-300 3 August 1998 page 37	Date Airline Registration
	Boeing 767-200 26 September 1981 page 144	Date Airline Registration
	Boeing 767-200ER 6 March 1984 page 144	Date Airline Registration
	Boeing 767-300 30 January 1986 page 144	Date Airline Registration
	Boeing 767-300ER 19 December 1986 page 144	Date Airline Registration
	Boeing 767-400ER 9 October 1999 page 144	Date Airline Registration
	Boeing 777-200 12 June 1994 page 93	Date Airline Registration

AIRCRAFT	MY FIRST FLIGHT		
Boeing 777-200ER 7 October 1996 page 93	Date	Airline	Registration
Boeing 777-300 16 October 1997 page 93	Date	Airline	Registration
Boeing 777-300ER 24 February 2003 page 93	Date	Airline	Registration
Boeing 787-8 15 December 2009 page 173	Date	Airline	Registration
Boeing 787-9 17 September 2013 page 173	Date	Airline	Registration
Boeing 787-10 31 March 2017 page 173 SPENCER BENNETT	Date	Airline	Registration
Bombardier Canadair CL44 15 November 1959 page 164	Date	Airline	Registration
Bombardier Canadair CL44D-4 16 November 1960 page 164	Date	Airline	Registration

	AIRCRAFT	MY FIRST FLIGHT
	Bombardier Canadair CL215 23 October 1967 page 153 ROGER SYRATT	Date Airline Registration
	Bombardier Canadair CL415 6 December 1993 page 153	Date Airline Registration
	Bombardier Canadair CL600 Challenger 8 November 1978 page 163	Date Airline Registration
	Bombardier Canadair CRJ 100 10 May 1991 page 76	Date Airline Registration
	Bombardier Canadair CRJ 200 13 November 1995 page 76	Date Airline Registration
	Bombardier Canadair CRJ700 27 April 1999 page 87	Date Airline Registration
	Bombardier Canadair CRJ900 21 February 2001 page 87	Date Airline Registration
	Bombardier Canadair CRJ1000 3 September 2008 page 87	Date Airline Registration

AIRCRAFT	MY FIRST FLIGHT		

Bristol 170 Mk1 Freighter
2 December 1945
page 170

Date	
Airline	
Registration	

Bristol 170 Mk32 Freighter
16 January 1953
page 170

Date

Airline

Registration

Bristol 175 Britannia 100
16 August 1952
page 120

Date

Airline

Registration

Bristol 175 Britannia 300
31 July 1956
page 120

Date

Airline

Registration

Britten Norman BN-2A Islander
13 June 1965
page 95

Date

Airline

Registration

**Britten Norman BN-2A MkIII
Trislander**
11 September 1970
page 139

Date

Airline

Registration

Comac C919
5 May 2017
page 74

WEIMENG

Date

Airline

Registration

Convair 990
24 January 1961
page 22

ROGER SYRATT

Date

Airline

Registration

	AIRCRAFT	MY FIRST FLIGHT
	Curtiss C46 Commando 26 March 1940 page 54 ROGER SYRATT	Date Airline Registration
	Dassault Breguet Mercure 28 May 1971 page 86 LEWIS GRANT	Date Airline Registration
	de Havilland Comet 1 27 July 1949 page 111	Date Airline Registration
	de Havilland Comet 4 28 August 1950 page 111	Date Airline Registration
	de Havilland Comet 4B 27 June 1959 page 111 BRIAN BICKERS	Date Airline Registration
	de Havilland Comet 4C January 1960 page 111	Date Airline Registration
	de Havilland DH114 Heron Srs 1 10 May 1950 page 77	Date Airline Registration
	de Havilland DH114 Heron Srs 2 14 December 1952 page 77	Date Airline Registration

AIRCRAFT	MY FIRST FLIGHT		
de Havilland DHC 2 Beaver 16 August 1947 page 122	Date	Airline	Registration
de Havilland DHC 6-100 Twin Otter 20 May 1965 page 81 ROGER SYRATT	Date	Airline	Registration
de Havilland DHC 6-200 Twin Otter page 81 JOHN BENNETT	Date	Airline	Registration
de Havilland DHC 6-300 Twin Otter May 1969 page 82	Date	Airline	Registration
de Havilland DHC 6-400 Twin Otter 1 October 2008 page 82	Date	Airline	Registration
de Havilland DHC 7 27 March 1975 page 56	Date	Airline	Registration
de Havilland DHC 8-100 20 June 1983 page 99	Date	Airline	Registration
de Havilland DHC 8-200 31 January 1995 page 99	Date	Airline	Registration

	AIRCRAFT	MY FIRST FLIGHT
	de Havilland DHC 8-300 15 May 1987 page 99	Date Airline Registration
	de Havilland DHC 8-400 January 1988 page 99	Date Airline Registration
	de Havilland DHC 8-Q400 page 99	Date Airline Registration
	de Havilland Dragon Rapide 17 April 1934 page 66	Date Airline Registration
	Dornier 228-100 28 March 1981 page 58 ROGER SYRATT	Date Airline Registration
	Dornier 228-200 9 May 1981 page 58	Date Airline Registration
	Dornier 328 6 December 1991 page 171	Date Airline Registration
	Dornier 328JET 20 January 1998 page 19	Date Airline Registration

	AIRCRAFT	MY FIRST FLIGHT
	Douglas DC1 1 July 1933 page 78	Date Airline Registration
	Douglas DC2 11 May 1934 page 78	Date Airline Registration
	Douglas DC3/DST 17 December 1935 page 176	Date Airline Registration
	Douglas DC4/C-54 14 February 1942 page 35	Date Airline Registration
	Douglas DC6 15 February 1946 page 36	Date Airline Registration
	Douglas DC6A 29 September 1949 page 36	Date Airline Registration
	Douglas DC6B 2 February 1951 page 36	Date Airline Registration
	Douglas DC8-10 30 May 1958 page 88	Date Airline Registration

AIRCRAFT	MY FIRST FLIGHT
Douglas DC8-20 29 November 1958 page 88 BRIAN BICKERS	Date Airline Registration
Douglas DC8-30 21 February 1959 page 88 BRIAN BICKERS	Date Airline Registration
Douglas DC8-40 3 June 1959 page 88 STEPHEN AUBURY	Date Airline Registration
Douglas DC8-50 20 December 1960 page 89	Date Airline Registration
Douglas DC8-61 14 March 1966 page 89	Date Airline Registration
Douglas DC8-62 29 August 1966 page 89	Date Airline Registration
Douglas DC8-63 10 April 1967 page 89	Date Airline Registration
Douglas DC9-10 25 February 1965 page 45	Date Airline Registration

AIRCRAFT	MY FIRST FLIGHT		
Douglas DC9-20 18 September 1968 page 46	Date	Airline	Registration
Douglas DC9-30 1 August 1966 page 45	Date	Airline	Registration
Douglas DC9-40 28 November 1967 page 45	Date	Airline	Registration
Douglas DC9-50 17 December 1974 page 45	Date	Airline	Registration
Embraer 110 Bandeirante 26 October 1968 page 156	Date	Airline	Registration
Embraer 120 Brasilia 27 July 1983 page 113	Date	Airline	Registration
Embraer 135 4 July 1998 page 117	Date	Airline	Registration
Embraer 145 11 August 1995 page 117	Date	Airline	Registration

	AIRCRAFT	MY FIRST FLIGHT
	Embraer 170 19 February 2002 page 39	Date Airline Registration
	Embraer 175 14 June 2003 page 39	Date Airline Registration
	Embraer 190 12 March 2004 page 39	Date Airline Registration
	Embraer 195 7 December 2004 page 39	Date Airline Registration
	Embraer E190E2 23 May 2016 page 83	Date Airline Registration
	Embraer E195E2 29 February 2017 page 83	Date Airline Registration
	Fairchild/Swearingen Metroliner 26 August 1969 page 128	Date Airline Registration
	Fokker F27 24 November 1955 page 167	Date Airline Registration

AIRCRAFT	MY FIRST FLIGHT		
Fokker F27-500 15 November 1967 page 167	Date	Airline	Registration
Fokker F28-1000 9 May 1967 page 75	Date	Airline	Registration
Fokker F28-2000 28 April 1971 page 75	Date	Airline	Registration
Fokker F28-4000 October 1976 page 75	Date	Airline	Registration
Fokker 50 28 December 1985 page 184	Date	Airline	Registration
Fokker 70 4 April 1993 page 168	Date	Airline	Registration
Fokker 100 30 November 1986 page 168	Date	Airline	Registration
Global Express 13 October 1996 page 163	Date	Airline	Registration

	AIRCRAFT	MY FIRST FLIGHT
	Grumman Gulfstream 1 14 August 1958 page 119	Date Airline Registration
	Handley Page Herald 25 August 1955 page 127	Date Airline Registration
	Handley Page Dart Herald -100 17 December 1958 page 127 DAVE WELCH	Date Airline Registration
	Handley Page Dart Herald -200 8 April 1961 page 127	Date Airline Registration
	Hawker Siddeley 748 25 June 1960 page 101 ROY CARTLEDGE	Date Airline Registration
	Hawker Siddeley Super 748 June 1979 page 101	Date Airline Registration
	Hawker Siddeley Trident 1C 9 January 1962 page 15	Date Airline Registration
	Hawker Siddeley Trident 1E June 1965 page 15	Date Airline Registration

AIRCRAFT	MY FIRST FLIGHT		
Hawker Siddeley Trident 2E 27 July 1967 page 15	Date	Airline	Registration
Hawker Siddeley Trident 3B 11 February 1969 page 15	Date	Airline	Registration
Ilyushin IL18 4 July 1957 page 107	Date	Airline	Registration
Ilyushin IL18B 30 September 1958 page 107 CHRIS CHENNELL	Date	Airline	Registration
Ilyushin IL62 2 January 1963 page 10	Date	Airline	Registration
Ilyushin IL62M 1971 page 10	Date	Airline	Registration
Ilyushin IL76 25 March 1971 page 53	Date	Airline	Registration
Ilyushin IL86 22 December 1976 page 181	Date	Airline	Registration

AIRCRAFT	MY FIRST FLIGHT
Ilyushin IL96-300 28 September 1988 page 146	Date Airline Registration
Ilyushin IL96M 6 April 1993 page 146	Date Airline Registration
Ilyushin IL114 29 March 1990 page 59	Date Airline Registration
Let 410 16 April 1969 page 65	Date Airline Registration
Let 410UVP November 1977 page 65	Date Airline Registration
Lockheed Jetstar 4 September 1957 page 138	Date Airline Registration
Lockheed L049 Constellation 9 January 1943 page 16 KARL MULLOCK	Date Airline Registration
Lockheed L100 20 April 1964 page 67 LOCKHEED MARTIN	Date Airline Registration

	AIRCRAFT	MY FIRST FLIGHT	
	Lockheed L100-20 1968 page 67	Date Airline Registration	
	Lockheed L100-30 August 1970 page 67	Date Airline Registration	
	Lockheed L188 Electra 6 December 1957 page 172	Date Airline Registration	
	Lockheed L649 Constellation 19 October 1946 page 16	Date Airline Registration	
	Lockheed L749 Constellation 15 March 1947 page 16	Date Airline Registration	
	Lockheed L1011-500 Tristar 16 October 1978 page 165	Date Airline Registration	
	Lockheed L1011 Tristar 16 November 1970 page 165	Date Airline Registration	
	Lockheed L1049 Constellation 14 July 1951 page 16	Date Airline Registration	

	AIRCRAFT	MY FIRST FLIGHT	
	Lockheed L1649 Starliner 10 October 1956 page 16 RALF MANTEUFEL	Date Airline Registration	
	Lockheed LM100J 25 May 2017 page 67 LOCKHEED MARTIN	Date Airline Registration	
	McDonnell Douglas DC10-10 29 August 1970 page 129	Date Airline Registration	
	McDonnell Douglas DC10-15 January 1981 page 129	Date Airline Registration	
	McDonnell Douglas DC10-30 June 1972 page 129	Date Airline Registration	
	McDonnell Douglas DC10-40 February 1972 page 129	Date Airline Registration	
	McDonnell Douglas MD11 10 January 1990 page 18	Date Airline Registration	
	McDonnell Douglas MD81 18 October 1979 page 150 ROY CARTLEDGE	Date Airline Registration	

AIRCRAFT	MY FIRST FLIGHT		
McDonnell Douglas MD82 8 January 1981 page 150	Date Airline Registration		
McDonnell Douglas MD83 17 December 1984 page 150	Date Airline Registration		
McDonnell Douglas MD87 4 December 1986 page 150	Date Airline Registration		
McDonnell Douglas MD88 15 August 1987 page 150	Date Airline Registration		
Nord 262 24 December 1962 page 182	Date Airline Registration		
ROMBAC 1-11 18 September 1982 page 124	Date Airline Registration		
Saab 340 25 January 1983 page 23	Date Airline Registration		
Saab 2000 26 March 1992 page 55	Date Airline Registration		

	AIRCRAFT	MY FIRST FLIGHT
	Shorts Belfast 5 January 1964 page 12	Date Airline Registration
	Shorts SD330 22 August 1974 page 125	Date Airline Registration
	Shorts SD360-100 1 June 1981 page 92	Date Airline Registration
	Shorts SD360-200 October 1985 page 92	Date Airline Registration
	Shorts SD360-300 February 1987 page 92	Date Airline Registration
	Sud Aviation SE 210 Caravelle 27 May 1955 page 84	Date Airline Registration
	Sud Aviation SE 210 Caravelle 1 14 May 1958 page 84	Date Airline Registration
	Sud Aviation SE 210 Caravelle 1A 11 February 1960 page 84	Date Airline Registration

AIRCRAFT	MY FIRST FLIGHT
Sud Aviation SE 210 Caravelle 10B 31 August 1964 page 84	Date Airline Registration
Sud Aviation SE 210 Caravelle 10R 8 January 1965 page 84	Date Airline Registration
Sud Aviation SE 210 Caravelle 11R 21 April 1967 page 84 STEVE RYLE	Date Airline Registration
Sud Aviation SE 210 Caravelle 12 12 March 1971 page 84	Date Airline Registration
Sud Aviation SE 210 Caravelle III 30 December 1959 page 85	Date Airline Registration
Sud Aviation SE 210 Caravelle VI-N 10 September 1960 page 85	Date Airline Registration
Sud Aviation SE 210 Caravelle VI-R 6 February 1961 page 85 KARL MULLOCK	Date Airline Registration
Sukhoi Superjet 19 May 2008 page 79	Date Airline Registration

AIRCRAFT	MY FIRST FLIGHT	
Tupolev TU104 17 June 1955 page 98 LEWIS GRANT	Date Airline Registration	
Tupolev TU134 29 July 1963 page 114	Date Airline Registration	
Tupolev TU134A 22 April 1969 page 114	Date Airline Registration	
Tupolev TU144 31 December 1968 page 185 MATT FALCUS	Date Airline Registration	
Tupolev TU154 4 October 1968 page 148	Date Airline Registration	
Tupolev TU204 2 January 1989 page 11	Date Airline Registration	
Tupolev TU214 17 August 2003 page 11 OSIPOV DMITRY	Date Airline Registration	
VFW 614 14 July 1971 page 108	Date Airline Registration	

	AIRCRAFT	MY FIRST FLIGHT
	Vickers 1101 VC10 29 June 1962 page 103	Date Airline Registration
	Vickers 1151 Super VC10 7 May 1964 page 103	Date Airline Registration
	Vickers V 630 Viscount 16 July 1948 page 109	Date Airline Registration
	Vickers V 700 Viscount 28 August 1950 page 109	Date Airline Registration
	Vickers V 800 Viscount 29 September 1956 page 109	Date Airline Registration
	Vickers V 810 Viscount 23 December 1957 page 109	Date Airline Registration
	Vickers V950 Vanguard 20 January 1959 page 20	Date Airline Registration
	Vickers V951 Vanguard December 1960 page 20 DAVE WELCH	Date Airline Registration

	AIRCRAFT	MY FIRST FLIGHT
	**Vickers V953 Vanguard** May 1961 page 20	Date Airline Registration
	**Yakovlev YAK40** 21 October 1966 page 152	Date Airline Registration
	Yakovlev YAK42 7 March 1975 page 52	Date Airline Registration

CHRONOLOGICAL LIST OF FIRST FLIGHTS

Chronological List
of First Flights

	DATE	MONTH	YEAR	AIRCRAFT TYPE	PAGE
1948					
	16	July	1948	**Vickers V 630 Viscount**	page 109
1949					
	27	July	1949	**de Havilland Comet 1**	page 111
	29	September	1949	**Douglas DC6A**	page 36
1950					
	10	May	1950	**de Havilland DH.114 Heron Srs 1**	page 77
	28	August	1950	**de Havilland Comet 4**	page 111
	28	August	1950	**Vickers V 700 Viscount**	page 109
1951					
	2	February	1951	**Douglas DC6B**	page 36
	14	July	1951	**Lockheed L1049 Constellation**	page 16
1952					
	16	August	1952	**Bristol 175 Britannia 100**	page 120
	14	December	1952	**de Havilland DH.114 Heron Srs 2**	page 77
1953					
	16	January	1953	**Bristol 170 Mk32 Freighter**	page 170
1954					
	15	July	1954	**Boeing 367-80**	page 178
1955					
	17	June	1955	**Tupolev TU104**	page 98
	25	August	1955	**Handley Page Herald**	page 127
	24	November	1955	**Fokker F27**	page 167
	27	May	1955	**Sud Aviation SE 210 Caravelle**	page 84
1956					
	31	July	1956	**Bristol 175 Britannia 300**	page 120
	29	September	1956	**Vickers V 800 Viscount**	page 109
	10	October	1956	**Lockheed L1649 Starliner**	page 16

DATE	MONTH	YEAR	AIRCRAFT TYPE	PAGE
1957				
4	July	1957	Ilyushin IL18	page 107
4	September	1957	Lockheed Jetstar	page 138
6	December	1957	Lockheed L188 Electra	page 172
16	December	1957	Antonov AN12	page 175
20	December	1957	Boeing 707-120	page 178
23	December	1957	Vickers V 810 Viscount	page 109
1958				
14	May	1958	Sud Aviation SE 210 Caravelle 1	page 84
30	May	1958	Douglas DC8-10	page 88
14	August	1958	Grumman Gulfstream 1	page 119
30	September	1958	Ilyushin IL18B	page 107
29	November	1958	Douglas DC8-20	page 88
17	December	1958	Handley Page Dart Herald -100	page 127
1959				
11	January	1959	Boeing 707-320	page 178
20	January	1959	Vickers V950 Vanguard	page 20
21	February	1959	Douglas DC8-30	page 88
19	May	1959	Boeing 707-420	page 178
3	June	1959	Douglas DC8-40	page 88
27	June	1959	de Havilland Comet 4B	page 111
29	October	1959	Antonov AN24	page 160
15	November	1959	Bombardier Canadair CL44	page 164
23	November	1959	Boeing 720	page 179
30	December	1959	Sud Aviation SE 210 Caravelle III	page 85
1960				
	January	1960	de Havilland Comet 4C	page 111
11	February	1960	Sud Aviation SE 210 Caravelle 1A	page 84
24	June	1960	Hawker Siddeley 748	page 101
10	September	1960	Sud Aviation SE 210 Caravelle VI-N	page 85
6	October	1960	Boeing 720B	page 179
16	November	1960	Bombardier Canadair CL44D-4	page 164
	December	1960	Vickers V951 Vanguard	page 20
20	December	1960	Douglas DC8-50	page 89

DATE	MONTH	YEAR	AIRCRAFT TYPE	PAGE
1961				
24	January	1961	Convair 990	page 22
6	February	1961	Sud Aviation SE 210 Caravelle VI-R	page 85
8	April	1961	Handley Page Dart Herald -200	page 127
	May	1961	Vickers V953 Vanguard	page 20
21	June	1961	Aviation Traders ATL.98 Carvair	page 100
1962				
9	January	1962	Hawker Siddeley Trident 1C	page 15
31	January	1962	Boeing 707-320B	page 178
29	June	1962	Vickers 1101 VC10	page 103
1	August	1982	BAe 146-200	page 135
13	August	1962	BAe/Hawker Siddeley 125	page 118
24	December	1962	Nord 262	page 182
1963				
2	January	1963	Ilyushin IL62	page 10
9	February	1963	Boeing 727-100	page 29
19	February	1963	Boeing 707-320C	page 178
29	July	1963	Tupolev TU134	page 114
20	August	1963	BAC 1-11-200	page 123
1964				
5	January	1964	Shorts Belfast	page 12
20	January	1964	Beechcraft King Air 90	page 21
20	April	1964	Lockheed L100	page 67
7	May	1964	Vickers 1151 Super VC10	page 103
31	August	1964	Sud Aviation SE 210 Caravelle 10B	page 84
1965				
8	January	1965	Sud Aviation SE 210 Caravelle 10R	page 84
25	February	1965	Douglas DC9-10	page 45
27	February	1965	Antonov AN22	page 47
20	May	1965	de Havilland DHC6-100 Twin Otter	page 81
	June	1965	Hawker Siddeley Trident 1E	page 15
13	June	1965	Britten Norman BN-2A Islander	page 95

DATE	MONTH	YEAR	AIRCRAFT TYPE	PAGE
1966				
14	March	1966	Douglas DC8-61	page 89
1	August	1966	Douglas DC9-30	page 45
29	August	1966	Douglas DC8-62	page 89
21	October	1966	Yakovlev YAK40	page 152
1967				
9	April	1967	Boeing 737-100	page 63
10	April	1967	Douglas DC8-63	page 89
21	April	1967	Sud Aviation SE 210 Caravelle 11R	page 84
9	May	1967	Fokker F28-1000	page 75
30	June	1967	BAC 1-11-500	page 123
27	July	1967	Boeing 727-200	page 29
27	July	1967	Hawker Siddeley Trident 2E	page 15
8	August	1967	Boeing 737-200	page 63
23	October	1967	Bombardier Canadair CL215	page 153
15	November	1967	Fokker F27-500	page 167
28	November	1967	Douglas DC9-40	page 45
1968				
		1968	Lockheed L100-20	page 67
18	September	1968	Douglas DC9-20	page 46
4	October	1968	Tupolev TU154	page 148
26	October	1968	Embraer 110 Bandeirante	page 156
	December	1993	Airbus A300-600F	page 157
31	December	1968	Tupolev TU144	page 185
1969				
9	February	1969	Boeing 747-100	page 33
11	February	1969	Hawker Siddeley Trident 3B	page 15
2	March	1969	BAC/Aerospatiale Concorde	page 50
16	April	1969	Let 410	page 65
22	April	1969	Tupolev TU134A	page 114
	May	1969	de Havilland DHC6-300 Twin Otter	page 82
21	May	1969	Antonov AN26	page 160
26	August	1969	Fairchild/Swearingen Metroliner	page 128

DATE	MONTH	YEAR	AIRCRAFT TYPE	PAGE
1970				
	August	1970	Lockheed L100-30	page 67
24	August	1970	Aero Spacelines Guppy 201	page 126
29	August	1970	McDonnell Douglas DC10-10	page 129
11	September	1970	Britten Norman BN-2A MkIII Trislander	page 139
11	October	1970	Boeing 747-200B	page 33
16	November	1970	Lockheed L1011 Tristar	page 165
1971				
		1971	Ilyushin IL62M	page 10
12	March	1971	Sud Aviation SE 210 Caravelle 12	page 84
25	March	1971	Ilyushin IL76	page 53
15	April	1971	Boeing 737-200ADV	page 64
28	April	1971	Fokker F28-2000	page 75
28	May	1971	Dassault Breguet Mercure	page 86
14	July	1971	VFW 614	page 108
1972				
	February	1972	McDonnell Douglas DC10-40	page 129
	June	1972	McDonnell Douglas DC10-30	page 129
28	October	1972	Airbus A300B1	page 157
1974				
15	April	1974	Airbus A300B2	page 157
22	August	1974	Shorts SD330	page 125
17	December	1974	Douglas DC9-50	page 45
27	December	1974	Airbus A300B4	page 157
1975				
7	March	1975	Yakovlev YAK42	page 52
27	March	1975	de Havilland DHC 7	page 56
4	July	1975	Boeing 747SP	page 106
1976				
	October	1976	Fokker F28-4000	page 75
22	December	1976	Ilyushin IL86	page 181

DATE	MONTH	YEAR	AIRCRAFT TYPE	PAGE
1977				
31	August	1977	Antonov AN 72	page 132
	November	1977	Let 410UVP	page 65
1978				
16	October	1978	Lockheed L1011-500 Tristar	page 165
8	November	1978	Bombardier Canadair CL600 Challenger	page 163
1979				
	June	1979	Hawker Siddeley Super 748	page 101
18	October	1979	McDonnell Douglas MD81	page 150
1980				
28	March	1980	BAe J31	page 57
1981				
	January	1981	McDonnell Douglas DC10-15	page 129
8	January	1981	McDonnell Douglas MD82	page 150
28	March	1981	Dornier 228-100	page 58
9	May	1981	Dornier 228-200	page 58
1	June	1981	Shorts SD360-100	page 92
3	September	1981	BAe 146-100	page 135
26	September	1981	Boeing 767-200	page 144
1982				
19	February	1982	Boeing 757-200	page 37
3	April	1982	Airbus A310-200	page 62
3	September	1982	Beechcraft 1900C	page 137
18	September	1982	ROMBAC 1-11	page 124
5	October	1982	Boeing 747-300	page 149
26	December	1982	Antonov AN124	page 183
1983				
25	January	1983	Saab 340	page 23
20	June	1983	de Havilland DHC 8-100	page 99
8	July	1983	Airbus A300-600	page 157
27	July	1983	Embraer 120 Brasilia	page 113

DATE	MONTH	YEAR	AIRCRAFT TYPE	PAGE
1984				
24	February	1984	**Boeing 737-300**	page 43
6	March	1984	**Boeing 767-200ER**	page 144
17	December	1984	**McDonnell Douglas MD83**	page 150
1985				
8	July	1985	**Airbus A310-300**	page 62
	October	1985	**Shorts SD360-200**	page 92
28	December	1985	**Fokker 50**	page 184
1986				
30	January	1986	**Boeing 767-300**	page 144
6	August	1986	**BAe ATP**	page 116
30	November	1986	**Fokker 100**	page 168
4	December	1986	**McDonnell Douglas MD87**	page 150
19	December	1986	**Boeing 767-300ER**	page 144
1987				
	February	1987	**Shorts SD360-300**	page 92
22	February	1987	**Airbus A320-100**	page 41
1	May	1987	**BAe 146-300**	page 135
15	May	1987	**de Havilland DHC 8-300**	page 99
15	August	1987	**McDonnell Douglas MD88**	page 150
9	December	1987	**Airbus A300-600R**	page 157
1988				
31	January	1988	**de Havilland DHC 8-400**	page 99
19	February	1988	**Boeing 737-400**	page 43
13	April	1988	**BAe J32**	page 57
29	April	1988	**Boeing 747-400**	page 71
28	September	1988	**Ilyushin IL96-300**	page 146
21	December	1988	**Antonov AN225**	page 180
1989				
2	January	1989	**Tupolev TU204**	page 11
20	June	1989	**Boeing 737-500**	page 43

DATE	MONTH	YEAR	AIRCRAFT TYPE	PAGE

1990

	DATE	MONTH	YEAR	AIRCRAFT TYPE	PAGE
	10	January	1990	McDonnell Douglas MD11	page 18
	1	March	1990	Beechcraft 1900D	page 137
	29	March	1990	Ilyushin IL114	page 59

1991

	10	May	1991	Bombardier Canadair CRJ 100	page 76
	25	September	1991	BAe J41	page 57
	25	October	1991	Airbus A340-300	page 154
	6	December	1991	Dornier 328	page 171

1992

	24	March	1992	BAe RJ85	page 135
	26	March	1992	Saab 2000	page 55
	1	April	1992	Airbus A340-200	page 154
	13	May	1992	BAe RJ100	page 135
	23	June	1992	BAe RJ70	page 135
	2	November	1992	Airbus A330-300	page 162

1993

	22	February	1993	McDonnell Douglas MD90	
	11	March	1993	Airbus A321-100	page 41
	4	April	1993	Fokker 70	page 168
	6	April	1993	Ilyushin IL96M	page 146
	6	December	1993	Bombardier Canadair CL415	page 153

1994

	12	June	1994	Boeing 777-200	page 93
	13	September	1994	Airbus A300-600ST Beluga	page 157

1995

	31	January	1995	de Havilland DHC 8-200	page 99
	11	August	1995	Embraer 145	page 145
	29	August	1995	Airbus A319	page 40
	13	November	1995	Bombardier Canadair CRJ 200	page 76

DATE	MONTH	YEAR	AIRCRAFT TYPE	PAGE
1996				
21	March	1996	**Tupolev TU214**	page 11
7	October	1996	**Boeing 777-200ER**	page 93
12	December	1996	**Airbus A321-200**	page 41
1997				
9	February	1997	**Boeing 737-700**	page 31
31	July	1997	**Boeing 737-800**	page 31
13	August	1997	**Airbus A330-200**	page 97
16	October	1997	**Boeing 777-300**	page 93
1998				
20	January	1998	**Dornier 328JET**	page 19
22	January	1998	**Boeing 737-600**	page 31
4	July	1998	**Embraer 135**	page 117
3	August	1998	**Boeing 757-300**	page 37
2	September	1998	**Boeing 717-200**	page 134
1999				
27	May	1999	**Bombardier Canadair CRJ700**	page 87
9	October	1999	**Boeing 767-400ER**	page 144
2000				
3	August	2000	**Boeing 737-900**	page 31
2001				
21	February	2001	**Bombardier Canadair CRJ900**	page 87
20	April	2001	**Antonov AN74TK-300**	page 132
23	April	2001	**Airbus A340-600**	page 154
2002				
15	January	2002	**Airbus A318**	page 40
11	February	2002	**Airbus A340-500**	page 154
19	February	2002	**Embraer 170**	page 39

DATE	MONTH	YEAR	AIRCRAFT TYPE	PAGE
2003				
24	February	2003	**Boeing 777-300ER**	page 93
14	June	2003	**Embraer 175**	page 39
17	August	2003	**Tupolev TU204-300**	page 11
2004				
12	March	2004	**Embraer 190**	page 39
7	December	2004	**Embraer 195**	page 39
2005				
27	April	2005	**Airbus A380-800**	page 68
2006				
13	October	2006	**Airbus A340-500IGW**	page 155
2008				
19	May	2008	**Sukhoi Superjet**	page 79
3	September	2008	**Bombardier Canadair CRJ1000**	page 87
1	October	2008	**de Havilland DHC6-400 Twin Otter**	page 82
2009				
5	November	2009	**Airbus A330-200F**	page 162
15	December	2009	**Boeing 787-8**	page 173
2010				
8	February	2010	**Boeing 747-8F**	page 28
20	December	2010	**Tupolev TU204-100SM**	
2011				
11	March	2011	**Boeing 747-8**	page 28
2013				
14	June	2013	**Airbus A350-900**	page 96
16	September	2013	**Airbus A220-100 (Bombardier CS100)**	page 140
17	September	2013	**Boeing 787-9**	page 173

	DATE	MONTH	YEAR	AIRCRAFT TYPE	PAGE

2014

| | 25 | September | 2014 | Airbus A320neo | page 142 |

2015

| | 27 | February | 2015 | Airbus A220-300 (Bombardier CS300) | page 140 |

2016

	29	January	2016	Boeing 737MAX8	page 24
	9	February	2016	Airbus A321neo	page 142
	23	May	2016	Embraer E190E2	page 83
	24	November	2016	Airbus A350-1000	page 96

2017

	29	March	2017	Embraer E195E2	page 83
	31	March	2017	Airbus A319neo	page 142
	31	March	2017	Boeing 787-10	page 173
	13	April	2017	Boeing 737MAX9	page 24
	5	May	2017	Comac C919	page 74
	25	May	2017	Lockheed LM100J	page 67
	19	October	2017	Airbus A330-900neo	page 151

2018

	31	January	2018	Airbus A321LR	page 142
	16	March	2018	Boeing 737MAX7	page 24
	28	April	2018	Airbus A350ULR	page 97
	19	July	2018	Airbus A330-700 Beluga XL	page 162
	6	November	2018	Airbus A330-800neo	page 151

Notes

Notes

Notes